TOKYO COMMUTE

TOKYO COMMUTE

Japanese Customs and Way of Life
viewed from the
Odakyū Line

By

A. Robert Lee

Line Compositions
by

Yuriko Yamamoto

RENAISSANCE BOOKS

FOLKESTONE, KENT

TOKYO COMMUTE
JAPANESE CUSTOMS AND WAY OF LIFE VIEWED FROM THE
ODAKYŪLINE
By A. Robert Lee

First published 2011 by
RENAISSANCE BOOKS
PO Box 219
Folkestone
Kent CT20 2WP
UK

Renaissance Books is an imprint of Global Books Ltd

ISBN 978-1-898823-06-3

British Library Cataloguing in Publication Data
A CIP catalogue entry for this book is available
from the British Library

Set in Bembo 11 on 12 by Dataworks, Chennai, India
Printed and bound in Malta by Melita Press

To
Pepa, Jess, Sacha

To
Hirohiko, Chihaya, Asagi

Acknowledgements

The writing of this text owes debts of a warmest kind to Mark Gresham and Shoko Miura who checked my Japanese usages and spellings, and to Nicholas Williams. Each has given generously of their own informed sense of Tokyo and Japan and made necessary suggestions for the text. I have also had the good fortune to be able to call on the following for inside information: Takeshi Onodera, Hirofumi Horikiri, Satoru Tsukamoto, Tomoko Kanda, Yuji Nakata, Teppei Kuruma, Yoshimi Hiroyasu, Kyoko Maeda, and James Vardaman. Other debts go to Maiko Chiba, Akina Sato and Sayaka Aoki. Thanks are especially due to Ruth Ozeki for her letter about the family connection with the Odakyū Line and to Paul Downey for the original of the Hakone Black Power image.

Yuriko Yamamoto would especially like to thank her Macintosh.

COVER PHOTOGRAPH by Josefa Vivancos-Hernández

Contents

1

Odakyū-sen

➲

Yōkoso! Welcome. Before you are the selective train timetables and chronicles of the good Line Odakyū, Tokyo, Japan. Odakyū-sen. OER, or in full, the Odakyū Electric Railway Corporation. Or rather one's own bit of the Odakyū Line and a whole circuit of thoughts and meditations that have gone with it. Journeys and journey metaphors. The Odakyū Line leaves Shinjuku Station, *Shinjuku-eki*, Central Tokyo, and heads southwest some 82.5 kms to end-of-the-line terminals in Hakone-Yumoto, Odawara, Enoshima and Karakida. An estimated 500,000-plus passengers board and de-board every day. The train appearances become quickly familiar: cream and blue carriages, newer grey-metallic carriages.

Plus the half-dozen Romance Cars, the sleek 'limited express' limousines of the line that ply at greater speed between Shinjuku and Hakone.

Twenty or so stops west along the Line is Mukōgaoka-yūen (to be precise nineteen by Local train, five by Express). My own station. If Shinjuku Station can be said to signify the metropolis, Tokyo as major city hub, then Mukōgaoka-yūen does duty as the home station. Mine, but I hope by implication, yours. Or so runs the

assumption in play. Wondrously ordinary at first sight but, as always, surfaces deceive.

Now an octogenarian, built in 1927, the Odakyū Line is currently being updated – new tracks and bridges and underground additions – between Yoyogi-Uehara, four stops out from Shinjuku, and Mukōgaoka-yūen. To any number of commuters at large, salaryman and increasingly salarywoman, schoolboy and schoolgirl, shopper and shopworker, and especially those travelling the morning and evening rush-hours, the Odakyu has acquired its own monicker. Affection-ately, and unaffectionately, its travellers reach for a not unfamiliar train image.

THE SARDINE CAN

Or in a local image
すし詰め
(Squashed Sushi)

The text's narrative has been written by yet another irritating Englishman Abroad, an *igirisu-jin*. Resident in Tokyo these past fourteen years. Teaching literature moreover. And at Japan's largest university. The Odakyū, then. Tokyo, then. Japan, then. And written through a current English-language lens. The line-illustrations are by Yuriko Yamamoto, Japanese by birth, a seasoned designer trained at Tama Art College, Kawasaki-shi, and working in the city. Her sketches and graphics give the Odakyū line an impressionistic register, a gallery of train, rail-track, station and environs pitched between photograph and pen-and-ink drawing.

Text and visual image together are offered as an imaginative interplay, an Odakyū Line, and with it a Shinjuku-eki and Mukōgaoka-yūen, of everyday to and fro, everyday east to west and west to east. *Odakyū-sen* has so been conceived as on-track and off-track observations. Mirrors. Musings. Memories.

A month-and-week sequence runs throughout, sixty items in all. These are meant as symptomatic Odakyū travel, together with days-out and evenings-out, a diary of other remembered rail-journeys, and even a 'creative' bibliography. The carriage scenes span vistas from the window, advertising posters, salarymen seated and standing, and women doing their make-up. Intersecting other Lines, by-lines as it were, come into play as does a gathering of notable Odakyū personalities. Narita airport is invoked along with a vista like that of the Tamagawa, the Tama River, between Izumi-Tamagawa and Noborito. The various tabulations are meant to serve as bas-relief,

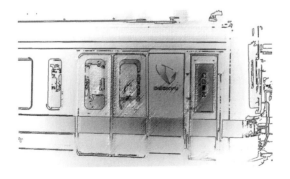

whether bags belonging to travellers, scenes inside or near Odakyū stations, local bike culture, haircuts, advertisements for salons or maquillage, variations of Odakyū colour-lines (blue especially), and the omnipresence of the *keitai* or mobile phone with overheard conversations. Train sounds are re-heard, not to mention how platform and on-board train staff operate. Travel grammar, travel noise.

The Odakyū-sen, to be sure, serves as but one of many train routes into and out of the metropolis, be it for job, office, store, eatery, movie or classroom. But it does so as always train theatre in its own right and, we hope, a marker for all other commuter train theatre – wherever train journeys are taking place.

Literary types schooled in eyes on the text close reading, or even latter-day fanciers of Barthes, Baudrillard or Derrida, will spot that what we have been about might be called cultural calligraphy. Hieroglyphs. Maybe just glyphs. To put *Odakyū-sen* undoubtedly among its Anglophone and America-phone literary betters, touchstones have been as various as *Canterbury Tales*, both Chaucer's and those of *A Canterbury Tale* (1944), the vintage Michael Powell-Emeric Pressburger movie. Accompanying literary footfalls look to John Dos Passos's *U.S.A.*, with its story-parallels and news extracts, David Markson's *This Is Not a Novel* with its antic author listings, and the TV scripts of the British playwright Dennis Potter. Given this is Japan there may also be distant recognition of home-grown journeying, that of the country's greatest poet, Matsuo Bashō, he of the classic pond-frog-splash *haiku*. Namely *The Narrow Road to the Interior (Oku no Hosomichi)*, first published in 1694, and aptly sometimes called travel-painting.

The text's sightlines, and indeed sounds, in turn are meant to call up different visual traditions. In Japan that might run from the wall art of the ancient Horyuji Temple in Ikaruga, Nara Prefecture, to the nineteenth-century woodblock prints of Utagawa Hiroshige, the great artist of *ukiyo-e* or the floating world. Who has not relished his *Thirty-six Views of Mount Fuji* (1832), not least the rising wave-and-Fuji composition? It might run from the birth of modern manga in the art of Osamu Tezuka (and *New Treasure Island* in 1947) to the walking-and-moving figure paintings of a contemporary artist like Masahiro Yamada. As to photographing trains in Japan, along with TV train documentaries and museums, that approaches a national pastime. Daily one sees cameras aimed at parked, arriving and departing trains, zoom lenses and tripods. A railway museum like that in Ohmiya (Saitama Ward, Tokyo), *Tetsudō Hakubutsukan*, and known familiarly as *Teppaku*, gives witness, every kind of track and station memorabilia. There is even a fond Japanese expression for boys who love trains – *tetchan*. In the west the murals of Diego Rivera and Thomas Hart Benton offer touchstones, along with the Victorian William Powell Frith's 'Railway Station', Harry Beck's landmark 1931 London Tube map, and a cubist American vignette like Mari-Louise van Esselstyn's 'The Escalator' (1942) – which became the cover for an earlier book of my own.

The upshot is an Anglo-Japanese rail-scroll. Or, in a tease of inter-active category, chap book and picture book, collage and montage. It might even be thought a FOLLY of sorts. Japan but also beyond-Japan in rail-time.

Embedded within the text's observations is the English repro-duced, and compositionally situated, of true-to-appearance Japanese usage: most of all as it appears on or around the Odakyū. It has become familiar lore that this can often sound awry, even a touch madcap. It can also be wholly endearing. *The Japan Times*, one of the capital's two English-language dailies (the other is the *The Daily Yomiuri*, though the *International Herald Tribune* publishes the *Asahi* as a Japanese English-language supplement) rightly quotes a Japanese observer as saying of some of the English-language usages – 'They sound more exotic…even if we don't (always) understand the actual meaning of the word'. A long-time Japanese friend suggests, again rightly, that 'public English is decorative, a kind of extra or trim-ming'. Much, too, as English may be Japan's official, or semi-official, second language, it has to be a necessary act of balance, and respect, to recognize how it takes its place inside Japan's own language with its subtly picturing *kanji* and its curvilinear *hiragana* and *katakana*. That poses the question of how this 'English' strikes the native Japanese-speaker? Words to catch no more than the ear, the eye, the attention? Words, however, that can, and when necessary often do, mean more? Japanese also vaunts its own name for the Western alphabet: *romaji*. Yet another 'language' to add to those already in play.

Whatever its aim or style, the lexical magic of Japanese English, Odakyū English, is invoked here with decade-long fondness.

**ODAKYŪ
LINE
ODAKYŪ
SEN
WORD
AND
SIGHT
SHINJUKU**

WORD
AND
SIGHT
MUKŌGAOKA-YŪEN
WORD
AND
SIGHT
WORD
AND
SIGHT

2

Shinjuku Station

➲

Shinjuku Station. The Odakyū's home terminal. Like Tokyo Station, Shibuya Station, and Ueno Station, one of Tokyo's great railway hubs. Quite its busiest. Indeed, reputedly, the world's busiest. Six railway companies. A dozen railway and subway lines. sixty-plus Entrances/Exits (*iriguchi/deguchi*). Fourteen major platforms. More than three million passengers overall. A.m. to p.m. Human motion and flow through its automatic ticket gates and stairways. Shinjuku-eki serves as train and train-change centre, a people centre, and a Japan centre. Etymologically: The New Inn. Other Shinjuku Lines, in equal rank with the Odakyū-sen, are part of JAPAN RAILWAY EAST. Known simply as the JR.

JR Lines
Chūo Main Line (Limited Express)
Chūo Rapid Line
Chūo-Sobū Line
Shōnan-Shinjuku Line
Saikyō Line
KEIŌ CORPORATION
Keiō Line
Keiō New Line

TOKYO METRO
Marounuchi Line

TOEI SUBWAY LINE
Toei Shinjuku Line
Toei Ōedo Line

Plus The Yamanote Line
The Circular Line of Tokyo

ODAKYŪ LINE
Shinjukū Station Departure
Two Levels
Ground level (3 Tracks 6 platforms)
Romance Car (Limited Express). Express.
Semi-Express. Rapid Express. Tama Express.
Sub-Ground Level (2 Tracks, 4 platforms)
Local. Section Semi-Express

ODAKYŪ LINE
Trains

ODAKYŪ LINE
Entrances
Day
Time

ODAKYŪ LINE
Exits
Day
Time

South
West,
East
New South

ODAKYŪ LINE
Rush-hour and off-peak
Weekday and Weekend
Day-time and Night-time
Tokyo travels
Japan travels
Nihonjin
Gaijin

Night
Time

GET YOUR TICKET

PASMO and **SUICA.** Twin all-purpose ticket-passes (regular tickets are *kippu*). Either will do (**PASMO** originally was issued by private companies like the Odakyū, **SUICA** by the Japan Railway or JR). Simply buy one and it can endlessly be renewed by paying in any amount. Renewable everywhere – stations, kiosks, vending machines. Besides travel you can use it to pay for newspapers, snacks, drinks, and stores will give you points from purchases to help recharge the card. Press 'English' on the ticket-machine screen and each service is available in your own language. Tokyo, to date, is the only major city where you can use these plastic beauties for all public transport. Not just the Odakyū but every train and bus-line in Tokyo. When you touch the pass-through station wicket with your card, the fare is deducted automatically and your balance comes up on the small monitor (with the letters **IC** – Intelligent Card). You can, to be sure, get one-off, one-journey tickets (prices all indicated

on the rail maps). There is even an art to how regulars put their ticket on to the screen-monitor. Some favour the hard bang-on-the-desk slap. Others go for something akin to a tennis-style lob. Small children reach up. Passengers with a touch of the librarian or civil servant about them place the pass on the screen with utter precision. Ticket gymnastics in small. Either way travel ease, travel comfort. Japanese ingenuity.

TICKET TO RIDE

FOLLOW THE SIGNS

PLATFORM READY

TIME FOR OFF

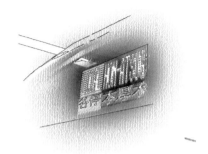

PUT YOURSELF IN THE DRIVER'S SEAT

TRAIN LEAVING

ADJUST YOUR FARE ON ARRIVAL IF NECESSARY

3

Shinjuku

And then there is Shinjuku itself, actually Shinjuku Ward, one of twenty-three in Tokyo. Huge interlocking world of commuters, youth, shoppers, entertainment, bars, eateries, passenger sidewalks and crossings. A meeting-place. A city beehive. Office skyscrapers to Dickensian back alleyways. Small counter noodle and *yakitori* places through to expensive cuisine restaurants (Japanese to general Italian-European). Rice-beef bowl shops like Yoshinoya. Salad and soup corners like Soup Stock Tokyo. Afternoon tea and cake retreats. An inevitable Starbucks. The Big Stores (*depāto*) of Times Square from the South Exit – most of them on the Southern Terrace – all come into view. Takashimaya. Lumine. Mylord. Flags. Isetan. Clothes and shoe boutiques by the score. Perfume and make-up franchises. Movies at Musashino-kan and each other Shinjuku cinema. Travel and holiday-booking through a company like *No. 1*, not to mention Odakyū Travel. The Shinjuku Washington if you want hotel fare. Case of Bordeaux or Burgundy? Try home-delivery from a wine store like Yamaya. You can do your kick-boxing here. Or ballroom dancing as filmed in *Shall We Dance?* – Koji Yakusho who plays Shohei Sugiyama, the dance-struck businessman, lives at Seijo on the Odakyū Line. On the Southern Terrace it was a huge pull when Krispy Kreme Doughnuts bowed in. Lines around the block and nothing if not a sugar threat to slim-line Japan.

West Exit gives you the serious hotels – Hyatt Regency, Keio Plaza, The Tokyo Hilton. Bus depot. Taxis stands. Bars. Yodobashi Camera with its electronics and computer treasury. Keio *depāto* (department store). It also gives you *omoide yokocho*, memory-lane, small alleyways of traditional Japan full of friendly eats and drinks corners. Nostalgia for many native Tokyoites. Round the corner from the East Exit there's Kabukicho with its 'pink' hostess bars, massage parlours and love hotels ('the water trade'), not to say relentlessly clanging pachinko parlours. Street-criers in high-coloured *happi* (three-quarter coats) advertising each and every ware, restaurant or club, games-centre or bar. Hints of *yakuza* and pimping. Schoolgirl

sexturf. Cruising males. If your taste so inclines there is gay Shinjuku ni-chōme.

Who could not have seen late-night-drinker Shinjuku, weaving salarymen, youth? Fresh from *sake* bars, restaurants, a host of watering holes. At no time more evident than after end of year parties, *bōnenkai* (literally forget the year). But this is Japan, almost no lout-violence, only the rarest conflict. It is also necessary observation that, around Shinjuku, you can see evidence of against-stereotype Japanese poverty. Street people. Sleeping inside cardboard boxes in the station was stopped by the authorities some time ago. But there is still the occasional huddled derelict or homeless person right amid the human speed of the commuters. Visible witness that all has not been The Bubble and Tokyo affluence. A yen-poorer, quite darker Shinjuku.

Morning and evening rushes. Bodies. Crowds. This or that commute. People. More crowds. Columns and weaves of bodies passing but rarely jostling each other. Daytime shoppers. Nighttime trippers. Ticket gates and barriers. Exits into daylight yield buildings against the sky. At night the same exits lead to street fare – sellers, neon, lights, surges of conversation. J-pop. Pachinko noise spilling into the air. As elsewhere in the city there are hustlers endlessly handing-out paper tissue packets with this or that advertisement or 'service'. Only more so.

All of it Shinjuku. All of it inside, or less than a street-crossing from, Tokyo's station of stations. And all of it, if it is your route, to be arrived at on the Odakyū-sen.

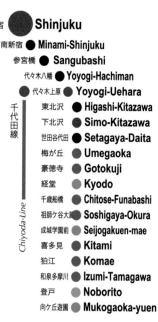

4

Mukōgaoka-yūen
North

➲

北

'I live in Mukōgaoka-yūen'
Japanese habit of saying your life *is* the station

Mukōgaoka-yūen etymology
'Up The Hill Park'

Classic local-station arena. First the station itself. Commuters. Odakyū ticket machines *(jidō kenbaiki)*. Pop-in/pop-out ticket gates *(jidō kaisatsu)*. Neat dark-uniformed office and platform personnel *(eki kakariin)*. And always passenger movement, passenger footsteps. Station dynamics.

Out front you have the taxi-ranks to the left (2010 minimum fare ¥710), a whole bus-complex to the right (stops, a depot, turn-arounds). Take a bus ride and you have two voices coming your way: a recording giving you the name of each stop and details of local stores or attractions and, alongside, the driver-conductor himself through his dashboard or head microphone. Is this a simply journeyman ride or local guided tour? On the west side (turn left) are the squares of bike-parking, meticulously geometric, and presided over by a team of older bike-guardians.

The inventory continues. A lottery kiosk plus music. An Odakyū-OX shop (newspapers, drinks, snacks). The ubiquitous and easy-to-use green phone to be found in or near all Odakyū stations (Shinjuku, Yoyogi-Uehara and Machida have batteries of four). ¥10 to get connected. A pitchfork of streets with small stores, eateries, banks, photography drop-off places, a pachinko parlour, a Mama-san bar. A Faculty bus-service for Meiji and Senshu universities atop the nearby hill though not available to students presumably on grounds of youth leg-power. The panorama could not be more familiar, ordinary, yet always with its own twist or play of angle.

HOUSING

Step out from the station itself and two architectures hit you smack in the iris. To the right you have a newly built 23-storey high-rise. No sooner built than occupied, laundry on the balcony, apartment lights at night. For sure a capital city has to house its people and where better than near a station, a Line, heading directly into Shinjuku? But this is also the vertical box par excellence, a built-environment at vertiginous and concrete right-angle to the Odakyū track. To the left there is an anomaly, a half-*minka*, half-modern Big House. Obviously under wealthy ownership. A banker, perhaps, a company boss? But it, too, was built only recently, and then − half-miraculously − literally moved sideways on grooves and wheels to make way for yet another standard housing block. It has a small garden *torii*, a stone lantern, *bonsai*-style shrubs, a vintage triangle roof, a surrounding wall made over from older walls. It also has a three-car garage, air-conditioning, central heating, and a waiting chauffeur each morning. New yet old. Next to the bike-parks and station walk yet redolent of a Kyoto or Nikko dynasty-residence.

Mix in every kind of other housing, high-rise and low-rise, off the road and near the road, and you have Mukōgaoka-yūen the dormitory yet Mukōgaoka-yūen the home. Not the least of this further hous-

ing is the vaunted 'mansion', less some Elizabethan country edifice or aristocratic Provençal homestead than, well, an apartment-block. Another box. Squat. And full of incoming electricity wires and cables. Each, too, has a killer name, something out of upscale housing fantasy – Famille Villa Tama, Grande Maison, Shangri-La, Casa Beruta, My Castle, Chateau Blanc, Tama City Heights and the like. There are also some sumptuous language jumbles as in Bell Face, Pre Rive, and (in

resounding capital letters) ARCCNCIEL. This latter, surely, French *arc-en-ciel*/rainbow spelling personified. *Le mot juste* indeed.

LEVEL CROSSING

Two. East and west. Classic Japan-crossings. Head towards the track just as the yellow, red and black barrier pole comes down. Then the pedestrian clan-gathering begins. You can be lucky and only one train will pass. But, Murphy's Law as you get tempted to think, it is a level crossing serial drama. The **Local** might approach, then its coming-from-the-other-way equivalent. Suddenly there are others. A *Rapid Express* or *Tama Express* (having come via the Chiyoda Line) that does not stop. Or one of the barrelling Romance Cars. Out pulls one of the **Locals**, but then arrives an *Express* or *Section Semi-Express*. Either way you are done for. Waiting for Godot. Lost in Space. Even when the way is clear, all trains out of range, there is always the possibility of another. So you scurry across, trying to keep to the left, one in a moving tail of bike-riders, shoppers, mothers-and-kids, students, children, older people. The fatal thing, well not exactly the really fatal thing, is if you hear the crossing's ping start up again, and you try to rush but almost get caught in what the French call *un accident a l'accordéon*. Meantime, on many a rain-free day, the drama is being photographed by a camera-enthusiast. Mukōgaoka-yūen Candid Camera. Mukōgaoka-yūen Brief Encounter. Odakyū by foot. Odakyū by eye and ear. All of them Level Crossings.

SUSHI

Like most Odakyū stations there is within a few paces a sushi place, one-counter and few tables. Run by a cheerful owner who, with his fellow sushi-wizards can lay before you a whole poetry of rolled fish-and-rice edibles. It is somehow less the food, good as that can be with due beer or *sake*, than the atmosphere. Intimate. An art of preparation and eating. Simply a corner place which will do duty for the thousands that help define Japan. Nicely lit but with shadow, a place to read the paper while wielding your *hashi* (chopsticks). Good for both solitary and companion dining. If you are from outside Japan you earn your true immigration-stamp here: a flourish of how to use to utter good purpose your acquired *domo arigatō* (thank you), *kudasai* (please) and *sumimasen* (excuse me), not to mention the chopsticks. Food for thought. Thought for food. Food and thought Japan.

SHRINE

Heading out from home towards Mukōgaoka-yūen North, and about five minutes from the station, you pass a small three-monkey

shrine. *Kōshin-toh*. Locals tell me that it is a Chinese-style harvest shrine in origin, actually a hundred years old and first put in place during the Meiji-era (1868–1912). As you look around at the ever more closely built residences it is hard to conjure up this area as one-time countryside – though there are still a few small ricefields and *nashi* (Asian pear) orchards a short walk away. The shrine two years ago was slightly relocated to make way for a latest *manshon* – that loan-word for a block of flats or *apāto*. Each new year on the Chinese lunar calendar (2008 was the Year of the Rat, 2009 the Year of the Ox) it is suitably given *shinto* dress: purificatory white paper zig-zags known as *gohei*, fruit, and emblematic plants like *habotan* – the decorative green-purple cabbage, *sumire* (violets), *botan* (peonies) and *deijii* (daisies). All to honour the crops, the process of the earth's growth and cultivation. It holds its place, however, a mere ceremonial bow away from block housing, the near-to-hand highway, any number of bike-parks, and the contrast of a day-and-night station on the Odakyū Electric Railway Line.

KINDERGARTEN

From time to time a stirring Mukōgaoka-yūen bit of Rousseau. Infants being happily transported in three or so carts. Each group, standing, holding the cart-edges, sport what might pass for a surgeon's round mini-hat (*bōshi*) in red, blue or green. *Irowake kyappu* or

separate colour caps. They are pulled along by the lady staff-members all in pinafores. Children out-for-a-walk-by the small river but not actually walking. The kindergarten, much to the point, has a name of winning syllabic complexity. *Akachan-Anshin-Onakama-Hoikushitsu* or Safe Place for Babies and Friends. Quite so. And when you see them out in their two or three carriage convoy the thought also comes into play that they might just be less about potty-training than train-training. Odakyū colts. Odakyū carriage-trainees. It is a lovely sight, not to say a lovely cacophony of whoops and cries by the children. Whatever else they are pre-keitai, unfettered of hand, ear and mouth as to phone.

NIGHTCLUB

Whatever else Mukōgaoka-yūen may be, it is not international casino or show-time, some infinitely to-scale Las Vegas or Monte Carlo. Especially as you exit from the North Side and meet it right next to nearby corner sandwich shops and several down to earth shorts-and-socks stores. Nor does it call up Tokyo *fashionista* playgrounds like Roppongi or Ginza, or even youth-ground like Harajuku. Even so, across the road, you are faced with a 'nightclub' using not one but

two names. GRAND OCEAN and STARMINE HIGH SOCIETY CLUB. The former uses vocabulary hinting of aquamarine ocean luxury and escape, the latter a showgirl's lone pink shoe etched next to the name. It is actually a salaryman's bar with girls who pour drinks, listen to domestic woes, earn extra yen, and then go back to being a student or OL (Office Lady). Or they act as confidants to visiting sociologists and novelists. The wonder of the place is its *chutzpah*. An Atlantic or Pacific ocean-liner does not come readily to mind, any more than does a hotel like The Sands or a setting for the latest 007 movie. A top mafia hang-out it is not, even though at night there are always smart-suited and waistcoated male personnel in the doorway. A ballroom for tuxedoed men or expensively gowned women, a roulette and blackjack betting palace, it is also not. So much said however, the club signs light up the night, opposite Mukōgaoka-yūen station, an engagingly distant reminder of our own local California or Mediterranean chic. Or, again, anything but. But lights there are, Odakyū night lights.

STORAGE

Take a slightly further stroll from the station and you come across a building-plot, if only for the moment, housing a square of corrugated white boxes. 3500 to 7000 yen per month in ascending sizes.

ABCDE. All of it like some whited sepulchre though constructed on black asphalt. The smaller units have door handles similar to the one on any house or shop. The bigger units have shutter-doors. As you enter there are drink machines either side – accompanied by the usual one or two eye-socket container for used cans. So it is a touch like a cut-down temple entrance. And the more you look the more the notion of storage resonates. Certainly there has to be more to it than a lock-up holding odd bits of furniture, a clothes-rack, a pile of old car-parts, even as I keep seeing, a pile of paint-cans and brushes used by a local house painter. Is this where Mukōgaoka-yūen itself is stored? Or, indeed, where all kinds of connected Odakyū history, even Tokyo and all Japanese history, is stored?

The Japanese instruction says STOP. Well anyone, you, myself, just might.

Worth getting a ticket to ride at any rate. And nothing other than a ticket to, or from, Mukōgaoka-yūen (minimum price ¥120), one which the barrier devours as you exit. Evidence of an Odakyū train journey that was, and then was not, while being at the same time good eco-practice. Not a hint of spare paper. Just the thing.

5

Mukōgaoka-yūen
South

➡

南

Out you step, a bit different from the North side. More commercial than the North, a shopping area. Greatly neon-lit at night. Taxi cabs, bus stops, a student gathering-place. Tissue handers-out, occasional pensioner-groups, and from time to time Jehovah's Witnesses with pamphlets. Live variety. Intersections.

DLK

In time-honoured Japanese usage **Dining room, Living room, Kitchen.** The whole esplanade is dotted with *fudōsan*, estate agents. Window after window of rental-offices advertise rooms, apartments, occasional houses. This is student turf so there are endless one-room or two-room units up for rent. They take their place close to any number of *izakayas* (lit. 'liquor store where you linger' or, in another version, a pub). Centre of the road is bike-parking where there used to be a monorail leading to the Mukōgaoka Amusement Park (Big Amusement Wheel, outdoor theatre, stalls, walkways). The Tsutaya store has floors of CDs, DVDs and videos. There are drug stores and a Games Centre with its youth pinball wizards. Small-rise buildings abound, one topped by a huge bowling-pin, another advertising 'The West of England College' (a one-floor language operation), a third the Jinke Trading Company. A mild uphill walk and you can visit Nihon Minka-en in Ikuta Park, a museum site of twenty or so reconstructed East Japan period houses, no small contrast with the shoe-boxes of modern Tokyo. Add yet other nooks and you have a whole if small-scale home and away – Mizuho and like bank-branches, coffee or doughnut shops, a *kōban* (small police office), flower shops, newspaper kiosks and optical stores, the shoe emporium **ABC-MART**, and the inevitable American fast-food, McDonalds (*makudonarudo*), KFC (*kentakkī furaido chikin*) and Jonathans (*jonasan*). DLKs. Shopping. Odakyū trains. Mukōgaoka-yūen. All yours.

BREAD-SHOP WITH PASTRY-AND-COFFEE CAFÉ

SCANDINAVIAN NATURAL ROMAN HOKUO (Since 1979). Viking loaves in Mukōgaoka-yūen? You select your bread or cake with a large pair of golden-coloured pincers with plastic orange handles, place everything on the tray, and head to the counter to pay. Hygiene worthy of a hospital operating theatre, even though on the outside parapet there is the faint inscription, a phrase to relish, **Scandinavia's Smell**.

Inside the shop, a wall-poster, you can read a BEST BREAD MESSAGE.

> We are Tomte. The Scandinavian region of northern Europe is the fabled home of gnomes called Tomte. Tomte love children. At night when everyone is sound asleep, Tomte go about casting magical spells to ensure the next morning's freshly baked bread will be especially delicious for the children. Cherishing the spirit

of the Tomte, we at 'Hokuo' take a highly skilled and gentle-natured approach to bread-making.

STORES

Two big ones, one Japanese-named and the other English-named. **Daiei** and **Life**. The former does clothes and household goods, bikes and shampoos, as well as groceries. Of late a truck engraved with the name of Gourmet Circus has taken to trading just outside the store entrance. **ZEST BAKERY** is how it bills itself with the following twice-over language-dough painted on the truck's sides: ***The secret of delicious is a thing flatly crushed when eating. The delicious source that exists so on the inside is spread in the whole.*** Irresistible. **Life** is mainly eatables and drinkables. Fruit and veg, fish, meat, milk, juice, cereals, its own in-house bakery, and an abundance of *bentos* (lunch-boxes). Just occasionally an assistant will take to hawking a store bargain, so you get an earful about reduced-price soba, must-go-immediately *tofu*, or a latest Kirin or Asahi beer. One item, however, can grate. As you head in, trolley before you, there's the smell of cooking sweet potato. Nothing wrong in that. But it is accompanied by a jarring and endlessly non-stop metallic jingle which can cause you to flee the adjacent fruit or greens counter. An auditory refugee. Some compensation, however, lies in when

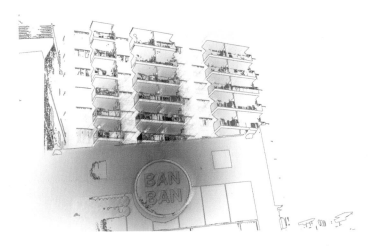

you pay. You get asked for your *pointo cādo*, the promise of percentage-deducted sweet potatoes by the cart-load.

PACHINKO

Trading under the name **Ban-Ban**. Good bit of onomatopoeia. Pass by, stick a nose in, and emanating as from all pachinko parlours you hear ear-splitting thumps as the machines race and pulse. Not to mention smoke: open a door and out pour whole columns of it. Tobacco smells to haunt eternity. Endless metal balls as the phrase goes. Plus the music, usually rock or J-pop. If you happen to win you go to a special window round the back to 'get your prize' – all to do with convoluted rules about gambling. But the colours are garish, the slots themselves full throttle lights-and-action electronics, and the punters themselves nothing if not wrapt and at peak seemingly as many as China's life-sized terracotta soldiers in Shaanxi Province. Japan without pachinko would be France without *boules*. **Ban-Ban** is but one of a number to hand. Pachinko's own Mukōgaoka-yūen.

6

Mukōgaoka-yūen Platform
North and South

⮞

Each platform a longitudinal island with tracks either side. If you're using the steps it's up to the overpass and then down. (Each step with parallel stripe in black, yellow, red and black – presumably to make sure the feet know just where they are even if you have a grip on either the metal handrail or the wall.) Plunge-prevention if you are going down, trip-prevention if you are heading upward. Four strips in all. The steps themselves are assiduously cleaned by green-overalled station employees. No danger of errant wrappers, a pile-up of dust or bird droppings. You can also go slow-motion and take the lift, or elevator (whose movement is akin to silent-running).

Yellow blind-strips throughout. Plus the usual arrow-indications of train.

Once on either platform you have the electronic train-timetable, a meticulously uniformed station man in white gloves wielding a mike-intercom, and a whole inventory of platform utensils. Fire

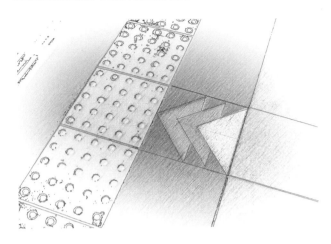

extinguisher. Water fountain. The Lifts or Elevators. A mirror for make-up adjustment. Plus those marked train positions for waiting – white triangle for **Local**, yellow triangle **Express** (you can also get one of the Romance Cars). Several wooden seats in park bench style. No-smoking signs. Station cameras at the platform ends looking like diagonally angled TV sets.

On both platforms, there is the Waiting Room, softly air-conditioned in the summer, softly heated in the winter. Eighteen fixed seats, nine to a side. Blue cushions. Slide doors. Top half all in glass. Operating-theatre effect. Just the place to get a quick glance at the newspaper. Time was when the south platform had a tiny four–five person *soba* counter under the stairs. Since it is traditional Japanese eating practice to slurp *soba*, it was a place to see, or equally hear, noodle-pleasure with accompanying ingurgitation acoustics.

A key centre of platform activities as you await your train is the Kiosk, or at least since there is only the one, that on the North Side.

The kiosk faces you like a grocery-cum-newsagent wall. OX SHOP (in blue) overhead. Pinafored lady assistant in charge. Layers or shelves of small-purchase items. Atop is a row of plastic-bag items: pens, lighters, mints, lip balm, cellophane wrapped tights, thin tubes of glue, tissue handkerchiefs and ever eye-catching portable ashtrays.

Plus square yellow packets of Calorie Mate Block, each a 'nutritionally balanced source of the energy needed for daily activities' for 'people-on-the go'. They look like shortbread, come in different flavours (cheese, cheesecake, chocolate, fruit, vegetable and potato), and feature in a Japanese TV commercial fronted by Kiefer Sutherland as

Jack Bauer of the prime time series *24*. The ad, of all places, and as though a mirror, takes place in a train carriage.

The counter itself is magazine city. Sports and fashion magazine, TV guides, cookery and IT publications and stacked manga volumes (many with girlie covers). One down and positioned at an angle to platform level are the newspapers. Those in Japanese like *Asahi Shimbun*, *Mainichi Shimbun*, *Tokyo Shimbun* and *Yomiuri Shimbun*, along with sports papers like *Hōchi Shimbun*, *Nikkei Sports* and *Daily Sports* whose front pages often boast a marvellous tabloid-garish front page. The three in English – *The Japan Times*, *The Daily Yomiuri* and *The Herald Tribune*. If any of these latter are unsold at 1.30pm, whether platform kiosk or the outside Odakyū–OX kiosk, they are whisked away. Other Odakyū stations keep them past 1.30pm until they are all sold. Obviously some distribution rite, but if you get there at 1.35pm or after, it can feel like an anti-Mukōgaoka-yūen newspaper conspiracy.

To the right is the OX SHOP Cooler with the usual beverages, coffee, tea, juice, and three varieties of bottled water. Portable liquids with a vengeance. But for myself the twin *pièces de résistance* are to be met with in two sublime names: **POCARI SWEAT** and **CALPIS.**

Pocari Sweat, *pokari suetto*, the blue and white can-label insists, is an ION SUPPLY DRINK. That is, originally, it was marketed as a sports drink to fight dehydration. **Calpis**, *karupisu*, like Pocari Sweat, has a slightly milky appearance, a light watery fruit or yogurt taste. You can get both in diet forms. Both are long-time Japanese drink standards. Both have names to seize the English-speaking attention. And, like local travel cocktails, both are to be seen in all Odakyū kiosks, all Japan kiosks. The kiosk, moreover, has various Odakyū Line cousins, more Ox-Shops or Odakyū Line Shops. Seijo boasts a particularly active one:

7

January Monday

➲

9 a.m. train out of Mukōgaoka-yūen. Rush hour. Station personnel push various Japanese rumps into the carriage. Faces are pressed against the door windows. You are in the middle, unable to move. Hands up to a strap. Claustrophobia threatens. Then, damn it, the train stops between stations. Slight delay. Apologies over the intercom – please be patient. What, in growing Poe-like incarceration panic ('The Premature Burial', 'The Cask of Amontillado'), do you imagine would be the alternative? This is the Odakyū as body-prison, travel sentence. Touch, smell, arms, all other body parts too close to others. Not fun. But then, once the train makes it to Kyodo, to Shimo-Kitazawa, to Yoyogi-Uehara, to Shinjuku itself, out you pour like lemmings given new life. Reprieved prisoners. Train relief.

Monday or any other day, few things more convey Japanese etiquette in miniature than the bow one passenger makes to those either side of the seat he or she is about to take. It is ceremonialism with a twist – considerate, often accompanied by the excuse-me of *sumimasen*. And then, with care, the body gets lowered into the seat and all become good carriage order. If a newspaper is to be read out it comes only to be vertically folded in the interests of discrete space-management, a small vignette of harmony.

Stunningly clear early afternoon. Keen chill but also sun. Waiting for the **Local** on Gotokuji Station it is possible to see Mount Fuji, *Fuji-san*, in all its snow-topped stateliness. If proof were needed of its iconic status, at once national and spiritual emblem, it lies in how fellow Odakyū passengers gaze lovingly upon its rising slopes even as the train slows into arrival. Stillness and motion. Zen and rail-track. Silence and brake-screech. It is a Japanese perfect configuration – sacramental mountain, skyline, train, travel. Platform contemplation.

Mukōgaoka-yūen rain-day. North Side entrance/exit (*iriguchi/deguchi*). One of the many etiquettes of the Odakyū-sen and other lines is the sight of a rack of free umbrellas (*kasatate*). They vary in quality and quantity – the cheapo see-though plastic kind and the better

one-colour or ornamental kind. But if you have forgotten yours, or
been caught out by a squall or worse, there they are. Miraculously
once the bad weather is past, they seem to return. Like some kind
of umbrella-lending library or umbrella cooperative. I continue to
marvel, even so, at how an overwhelming number of Japanese passengers always seem to know just when to bring their own umbrella.
Can it be as simple as that they are glued to the night before's TV
weather forecast? I keep thinking it must be ancestral village DNA,
like using straw, growing rice, making soba noodles, or knowing the
right degree of forward bow.

    Coming of Age Day (*seijin no hi*). Second Monday of January.
At Noborito three young women board in *furisode* (ultra-decorative
long-sleeved kimono), en route, evidently, to a local ward or shrine
celebration. They each look stunning, kimono-colours, hair up, *zori*
or circumflex-shaped slippers, white ruff. Each carries a small handbag or pocket-book suitably mascotted. They are now, at twenty,
legal to vote, smoke, drink, not to mention give sartorial splendour
to the Odakyū Line.

8

Odakyū Notables

➲

TARO OKAMOTO (1911-1996)

Mukōgaoka-yūen's own. Well almost. Japan's Picasso as often called. Painter. Sculptor. One of the nation's best known art-moderns. The offspring of celebrated parents – his mother, Okamoto Kanoko, the tanka-writer and novelist of *The Dying Crane/ Tsuri ha Yamiki* (1931) and *Portrait of an Old Geisha/ Rogistō* (1938) and his father, Ippei Okamoto, admired manga cartoonist. Born in Kawasaki-shi, raised in Tokyo's Aoyama District, these parents took him to both Europe and America – even as he launched himself as an oil-painter. Why Mukogaōka-yuen? Because not a township mile from the station in parkland is the Taro Okamoto Museum. 'Art is explosion', 'Art is magic', became Okamoto's manifestos. Both track back into his modernist-surrealist apprentice years. Fellow-expatriate Parisian alongside Picasso *lui-même*, Mondrian and Kandinsky, and drawn to the sway of Gaudí, Breton, Max Ernst, Louis Aragon.

Japan-returnee in 1941 on account of the war, his work proliferates, ever the vital presence – and in 1991 he gives 352 pieces of his brilliantly coloured paint and sculpture creations to Kawasaki-shi. Hence the creation of the Museum, and in Mukōgaoka-yuen. Within walking distance of the Odakyū Line, hence Okamoto's Mukōgaoka-yūen.

Fame most came his way with the iconic *Tower of the Sun*, the dish-like solar face and outspread wings which became the signature of Osaka's Expo 1970, the first world fair held in Asia. It compares with the octopus-legged figure in the Mukōgaoka park, another sculptural upright with raised white wing-arms, or the street-side sunflower faces in up-market Omotesandō (Chiyoda Line from the Odakyū). But no train-connection now better serves than Okamoto's 'Myth of Tomorrow' (*Asu no Shinwa*), his huge apocalyptic mural first painted in Mexico in 1967 in the style of Diego Rivera and the other great Mexican *muralistas* and as of November 2008 installed in Shibuya Station. An exploding human body at its centre with footfalls of Hiroshima/Nagasaki, if not all warfare. Splinters of colour. A raptor bird head. Rivulets of blood red. A memorial. A warning. Take the Odakyū to Shimo-Kitazawa, board the Inokashira Line, arrive at Shibuya. And before you, walled, massive, striking, is Japan's 'Guernica'. Nothing less.

AKIRA KUROSAWA (1910-1998)

Does Japanese film look to a more personifying name? If you have heard of Tokyo, taken a remotest interest in great cinema, you have heard of Kurosawa. But to be aboard the Odakyū is to win a small increment of magic. That is if you are heading through Seijogakuen-mae. Seijo it is where, at home and at the Toho Studios, Kurosawa did his picture-boards, pondered each Tokugawa shōgun and samurai story-line, and plotted his camera moves. Every frame a study. The Odakyū so gets you within a director's hail of where his best art was sieved and served. No matter that he was born in Omori in Ota Ward. Here, with his actress wife Yoko Yaguchi, this screen perfectionist – oddly tall for a Japanese – ate and lived and made cinema. A Seijo resident. An Odakyū user. How to call up the Kurosawa of the screen? Maybe the early black-and-white *Rashōmon* (1950), with its medieval setting and four competing versions of a killing, a rape, and husband and wife truth. Maybe the great Shakespeare-inspired epics, *Throne of Blood* (*Kumonosu-jō*), from *Macbeth*, with one of the greatest ever on-screen deaths as the usurper protagonist Washizu Taketori is executed by that hail of arrows from his own troops. Or the five years in the making *Ran*, from *King Lear*, with its stunning choreographies of battle ranks and human passion. Inevitably any of these or others with the mighty Toshirō Mifune come into play, whether *Sanjuro* as the chronicle of the seasoned but (by definition) master-less *rōnin*, or Y*ojimbo* as the portrait of the lone bodyguard figure to whom Sergio Leone/Clint Eastwood's later no-name western gunman owes everything. Or, to be sure, *The Seven Samurai*, the warrior-village alliance against marauders with due *bushidō* chivalry caught to visual perfection. Classic swordsmanship tied into human ambiguity. Life tied into death. Above all the genius of Kurosawa's camera-eye. Whether one has travelled also by London Tube, Paris Métro, New York Subway or Moscow Underground to see on-screen Kurosawa, the Odakyū – and Seijo – is where he himself travelled. A train privilege to be that close.

JIRO SHIRASU (1902-1985)

Key political and cultural figure in the making of post-war Japan. Rich. Stunningly handsome-elegant. Diplomat and businessman. He notably stood up to Douglas MacArthur as Japan was being re-fashioned – 'Japan may have lost the war but I don't remember becoming slaves.' For this he became known as 'the difficult Japanese', 'the most insubordinate Japanese ever known'. As the nation surveyed itself in ruins, he drove a Bentley, later a Porsche. The charm, the grandeur, it was sometimes called dandyism, owed much to the fact that he was both a kind of Japanese 'English Gent' and, at the same time, a kind of Japanese 'Yankee'. The former had much to do with the manicured English he acquired in the half-dozen years spent at Clare College, Cambridge, the latter with having become the first well-known figure in Japan to have been seen publicly wearing jeans to the amazement of the elite cadres and the general populace. He early became an ally of, then aide to, Prime Minister Shigeru Yoshida (PM May 1946-May 1947, 1948-1954 – his grandson Taro Aso would become PM in 2008) and acted as liaison to MacArthur. A key player, in the US and Japan conferences, for his input into the 1946 Peace Constitution, and a key player in holding out for Japanese dignity in the face of defeat. There was the marriage to Masako Shirasu (1910-1998), stellar art-collector, story-writer, and Noh expert. The pair of them continue to signify Japanese Camelot. High politics, high fashion. There was, and still is, the house to match – Buaiso – where they moved in 1943. Where? Near the Odakyū Line's Tsurukawa, five stations west of Mukōgaoka-yūen and two before Machida.

A one-time farmhouse, it is now a museum visited by royalty and commoner alike. And then there was *the* photograph? Taken in 1951, black and white, it recurs in culture-collections, galleries, magazines. Shirasu, a fifty-one-year-old of landed Japanese stock, is seated next to his wife in what might be a film director's chair. Jeans indeed (and rolled at the cuffs). T-shirt. Cigarette in hand. One leg insouciantly over the other. Composed in his informality. One of the most iconic photo-portraits in post-war Japanese culture. Power, style. Handsome to a fault. At ease in a Japan both of East and West. Odakyū-ease. In 2009, NHK made him the subject of a two-part documentary, in both English and Japanese.

KAORI MIHASHI (1976–)

Odakyū as crime mystery or at least crime setting? At its centre *barabara jiken*, literally 'scattered parts incident'. Kaori Mihashi, the battered wife who in revenge took a wine-bottle to the head of her drunken, abusive husband, then sleeping, and sawed his corpse into five parts. Each she deposited around Tokyo, Shinjuku and Shibuya wards, filing a Missing Person report at the Yoyogi Police Station. Gothic revenge. One of the parts, Yosuke Mihashi's head, went to a park in Machida – transported how? By the Odakyū Line? And in one of the bags like those later itemized here in *Tokyo Commute*? Thoughts of Kevin Spacey's John Doe character in the film *Se7en* (1995). She and her husband were fairly high-rollers, an apartment in an eleven-storey Shibuya condominium, good jobs (he working for the securities firm of Morgan Stanley), married since 2003. But, as the court proceedings would reveal before Kaori Mihashi received her fifteen-year sentence from the Tokyo District Court, it was an unhappy, violent alliance. In June 2005, she went to a hospital with a broken nose and facial wounds. Both had affairs. Fights, choking, noise, flounces in and out. The psychiatrists argued for trauma (PTSD) on her part, the daughter of affluent parents but disciplinarian father who as a company president was used to giving commands. The husband was said to accuse the wife of not being equal to his self-vaunting high salaryman status. She, allegedly, craved the still better, moneyed life. All the stuff of tabloids.

Day upon day actual reality TV. There was linkage to other recent and actual Japanese figures of murder-gothic. Joji Obara, jailed for life as a serial rapist and likely drugs and rape killer of Lucie Blackman (and two other women), a young British woman working as a hostess in Roppongi. Her dismembered body parts were found in a cave near

Miura, Kanagawa. The schoolboy in Nara who burned down the family house killing his stepmother in pique at his physician-father's demand that he do better at school. The twenty-one-year-old Yuki Muto who killed and cut up his sister in Shibuya because she taunted him about not making it to dental college. This is a Japan against the grain, inward, torqued. And one cannot but think of Kaori Mihashi, just maybe, buying that Odakyū ticket, bag in hand.

TSUYOSHI KITAZAWA (1968–)

A name from the Odakyū sports-stable. Machida born and raised soccer star, a nationally known midfielder. Fifty-nine Caps, but only three goals scored. He played first for Honda FC (1987–1991), then – all one club despite the name-changes – Yomiuri FC (1991-1996), Verdy Kawasaki (1996-2000), Tokyo Verdy (2001-2002). Member of Japan's victorious 1992 Asia Cup team but also of the 1994 team that failed to qualify for the FIFA cup. His record, on most reckoning, is good but not great. Even his old Tokyo club website faint-praises him as 'not blessed with talent but determined to succeed'. Fred Varcoe, however, the veteran *Japan Times* sports editor, once called him a 'useless soccer player'. But since his playing career's end in 1992, he has emerged as one of the presiding faces and voices of Japanese soccer.

Why? Broadcasting. TV and radio. Whenever Japan is involved in a major competition, there he is, a voice fast becoming as familiar to Japanese sports-listeners as Howard Cosell to Americans or John Motson to Britishers. In 2006, for the World Cup he took over from the veteran commentator Jon Kabira. Plus he serves as a formally-nominated ambassador for the Japan Football Association, has brought soccer clinics to Cameroon and South Africa, and is a speaker for the grandly titled Football Communication Academy. Kitazawa-san is more than one of TV's *tarento*, those endless games panellists and studio fluff types whose role is simply to use up time. Which is not to make him one of broadcasting's heavyweights. 'Famous all over town' as the phrase runs. A contemporary media presence. And an Odakyū presence: think of all those schoolboy and after games trips, those bags of sports paraphernalia. Boots. Socks. Shorts. Shirts. Laces. Vaseline. Soccer travel. Soccer Odakyū.

RUTH OZEKI

She brings a truly distant Odakyū connection to bear: a *sansei*, American-born, living in Canada. Smith College and then Nara

University. The author of two consequential fictions. *My Year of Meats* (1998), America and Japan, in the form of two women's friendship, wittily portrayed as 'eating disorder' cultures, and *All Over Creation* (2003), modern pastoral centred in an Idaho potato farm in an age of genetic engineering and agribusiness. She and I met in Oakland, California, as fellow prizewinners of the American Book Award in 2004. Talk turned to Tokyo during which she mentioned her own Odakyū Line trips to Gotokuji-eki, one station away from Kyodo. A stop on all Local trains.

On request she came through with a memory-letter. An Odakyū Line memory-letter as it were.

My family's ancestral home is in Gotokuji. It belonged to my great-great-grandfather, who lived there during the Meiji Period. It's possible that earlier relatives lived there before him, but I don't know the history that far back. The home is located on property belonging to Gotokuji. My grandmother had inherited the multi-generational lease from the temple; however, since my mother and I were her only surviving relatives and we lived in the USA, she gave the lease to her nephew and niece. They were my first cousins-once-removed, but I called them Ojisan and Obasan. The first time I met them was in 1963, when I was seven years old.

My memories of that trip and of Gotokuji are vivid but confused. The old house didn't have a bath, or perhaps my Obasan just enjoyed the *sento*. One evening, on the way home, I heard a mewing sound coming from the sewer. There were deep open

sewage drains along the sides of the road back then, and way down at the bottom I spotted a wet box full of kittens that someone had tried to drown. I was horrified, and I begged my mother to let me climb down and save them and take them home. Of course she didn't let me. I cried all the way home. I thought she was the most heartless person in the world.

My Ojisan is now dead, but my Obasan is alive, and I still visit her and her children, who are my second cousins, from time to time. About twenty-five years ago, they tore down the original old house and built a modern multi-family apartment building, so there are three generations and eleven or twelve of my relatives living there now. My Obasan never fails to remind me that the property should, by rights, have been mine, and had it not been for the kindness of my grandmother, they would not have a home. She is very generous to acknowledge this old debt, but her gratitude is unnecessary. She looked after my grandmother in her later years, and her family has always made me feel at home when I visit Tokyo, so I am grateful to all of them.

9

Odakyū Line Sounds Familiar

➡

Train announcement recording in Japanese: 'Mukōgaoka-yūen desu'.

Then the English recording: 'The next station will be Mukōgaoka-yūen'.

Third time by conductor (guttural, throaty, choked): 'Mukogaōka-yūen desu'.

Er...yes, got it.

Keitai denwa. Phone-talk. Hand-over-mouth 'Hai, hai' (Yes, yes), 'Honto ni?' (Really?), 'Kawaii!' (Cute!), 'Uso!' (Is that true?). 'So… so…so…so.' (So..so…so…so). Plus affirmative head nods.

Sudden ring tones, with follow-up conversation, under sign saying 'Please switch your phone to manner mode'.

Yellow straps supposedly indicating a quiet zone – but phone talk continues and, well, the straps? Creak in sync with the train's sway.

Buzz-hum of young Japanese earplug music.

Sleeper's snore, gentle or loud, plus head landing on next passenger's shoulder.

Male throat-clearing. Serious throat-clearing. Sneezes. Coughs.

Women's laughter, more hand over mouth.

Winter-time sniffing (no nose-blowing). Gauze masks.

Strap creak as train sways.

Rustle of vertically folded newspapers.

Snap of shaded carriage blind being pulled down (or up).

Whack of umbrella (especially if wet) falling on floor.

Static-affected train and platform announcements.

Whoosh of slide-doors opening and closing.

Carriage courtesy-language: *arigatō gozaimasu* (thank you), *sumimasen* (excuse me), *gomen-nasai* (I'm sorry), *do itasi-mashite* (you're welcome).

Announcements. Once in a while you get the one arrival or departure recording played simultaneously with another. An overlap ear-confusing enough. But then, not infrequently, the platform guard will also get in on the action. Three voices, thus, operate and vie. Almost akin to a group of unstoppable talkers each hammering home their fixed position on the world.

Which leads on to another key Odakyū sound feature: the train vocalizations of the platform staff. Known as *kanko ōtō* – call and response. At every station, or from the driver's cabin, you hear an affirmatory call. Train stopping. Brake. Acknowledgment of the conductor's bell. The number of carriages in the train. All followed by *yoshi* (OK). This comes over as the monosyllable *yosh*. The staff themselves, platform and aboard, also use an arm-pointing system, right and left, as if to further affirm the train's movement. Experts explain that this is all a way of keeping alert, focus, a system of error prevention designated *shisa kanko*. Any journey thus becomes yet another ritual platform. Driver and guard train-phonetics. Odakyū speech-communication class. Odakyū Electric Railway repertory theatre.

10

Train Notices

ODAKYŪ LINE

Be careful in case of an emergency stop being
made to avoid an accident

This window cannot be opened.

Please set mobile phones on
'manner mode' and refrain
from speaking on phones

Please carry backpacks in your
arms or put them in the luggage rack

Please allow enough space for
others to sit

TOZAI LINE (UNCLAIMED PERSONS)

Please inform the station staff or train crew
immediately if you notice any suspicious
unclaimed objects or persons in the station
or on the train.
Thank you for your cooperation

YAMANOTE LINE (EXPECTING YOUR MOTHER)

Doors on this side will open
Doors on opposite side will open

There are priority seats reserved for elderly passengers,
handicapped passengers, expecting mothers and passengers
accompanying small children

KEIO LINE (CLOSE-UP KINDNESS)

Please refrain from using Mobile Phones
Hold your bag
Please sit close to others
Thank you for your kindness

ODAKYŪ LINE (METERING)

Make your way to the stairs 50 meters
Buy a Limited Express Ticket 70 meters
Take the Elevator 90 meters
Call of Nature? 2nd Floor-distance unspecified (so hurry)

11

Odakyū Commercials

➲

O PANASONIC!
PANASONIC – IDEAS FOR LIFE
HELLO! PANASONIC

TOYOTA – DRIVE YOUR DREAMS
TOYOTA NETZ – MAKE THE STYLE

HONDA – THE POWER OF DREAMS
DO YOU HAVE A HONDA?

MITSUBISHI MOTORS – Drive@earth

NEC – EMPOWERED BY INNOVATION

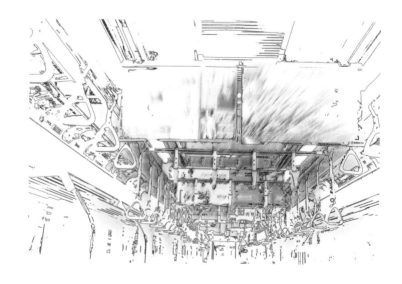

CANON – EVERYDAY PHOTO!
MAKE IT POSSIBLE WITH CANON

HITACHI – INSPIRE THE NEXT

BRIDGESTONE – LET'S GREEN DRIVE
BRIDGESTONE – PASSION FOR EXCELLENCE

TOSHIBA – LEADING INNOVATION

BRAUN – MORNING REPORT

PHILLIPS – SENSE AND SIMPLICITY

AU BOX CD, LISMO – PAINT IT MUSIC

NISSAN – THE WAY YOU MOVE
NISSAN CUBE, MINI MPV – I'M PEACEFUL

EPSON – EXCEED THE VISION

DOCOMO (Phones)

Style Series, Prime Series, **Smart Series, Pro Series**

SONY – like. no. other

12

February Tuesday

➲

Not the least part of Odakyū travel has to be the Fare Adjustment Machine. *Seisan ki.* You underpaid for your ticket – the upshot is that if you put it in the automatic gate the warning-ping goes off with a small red light flashing. So, a quick sidestep to the FAM (as it might be called). In goes your ticket. Excess price shows up on the screen. Due money is inserted. Out comes another ticket which will do the trick. You then exit from the station, un-troubled, un-guilty, and with quite none of the grief that can follow with a Western ticket office or inspector. Every station in the world should have one. Every home should have one.

Roof-top vistas en route from Mukōgaoka-yūen. The train rides high, and through the window or door window-panel, you get to see upper-level Kanagawa housing. Four items. First, just after Chitose-Funabashi, there's HORIZON CHAPEL in bold green lettering. Heaven's Gate Odakyū? Second, near Kyodo, DOVER HOTEL. Is it a love-hotel, a business hotel, even a left-over sign *à la Gatsby*? Third, KONAMI SPORTS CLUB just before Shimo-Kitazawa, with a swimming pool as main feature. There you are on the crowded morning train, barely awake, eyes half-open, and you see someone mid-air doing the likes of an Olympic double-twist. Fourth, the JAMII MOSQUE, within hailing distance of Shinjuku, high white minaret and dome golden in the light – nice contrast with each Buddhist or Shinto temple spire. Built, I discover, by Turkish Muslims in the 1930s, demolished in 1986, and handsomely rebuilt and opened in 2000. It is early morning and the mind wanders. Can this still be Odakyū Japan?

Sweet sight. School-aged couple, both in school uniform, sharing white ear-plugs for an iPod, an MP3 player. They look like they are joined by some Y-shaped umbilical stethoscope. You can just about hear it is J-pop (or even, as of late, J-hop), and not least as they both make a slight sway to the rhythm. Lots of eye-gazing. Obviously early passion, love. Discreet. Japanese-style. Off they get at Noborito, ear-to-ear and one white wire for each. Music connected. Hormone connected.

Eki-bento. Railway lunch-box, and nowhere at its more character-istically inviting than Shinjuku Station. Within reach of the Odakyū exits, Shinkuju South and Shinjuku West, you have various kiosk-shops. Hygienic light-wood box, elegant wrapping, and a selection of eatables artistically composed upon a bed of rice. Prawns (*ebi*), fish (mackerel or a white fish like *tai*), chicken, *tofu*, various species of pickle, vegetables typically sautéed or dressed in sesame-seed *konny-aku* (water plant). Occasionally eel (*unagi*) or *sushi*. Dark red pickle-plum. Packeted soy. Green serrated-edge paper as food dividers. The whole set out as an edible mosaic upon the underlying rice. Chop-sticks (*hashi*) always included. This is travel cuisine largely associated with the *shinkansen*, the longer route. But it will do for the office, for anyone's work. Food to quell any appetite. Japan's food.

Hallelujah! Today, for the first time I can remember, a female voice took to making the intercom and train-stop announcements. There have been the occasional platform personnel previously. But a female voice, and without the usual strangulated male-voice texture, this is a true break with tradition. 'Girls don't do trains' has long been the accepted mantra. Train driving, guards on the platform, engineers, repair crews – is not that boy-into-men fare, be it Tokyo, the Odakyū, or far beyond. Odakyū feminism has yet to make, shall we say, its full bow.

13

Odakyū Keitaispracht

➲

I'm on the train. The Local.
今、各駅停車の中です。
Ima kakueki teisha no naka desu.

We're just leaving Mukōgaoka-yūen.
向ヶ丘遊園を出たところです
Mukōgaoka-yūen wo deta tokoro desu

I'm changing on to the Express at Seijo.
成城で急行に乗り換えます。
Seijo de kyuko ni nori kae masu.

Damn. The train has stopped. There's some kind of delay.
くそ、電車が止まった。遅れそうだ。
Kuso. Densha ga tomatta. Okuresoda.

Won't be long. We're in Gotokuji.
豪徳寺にすぐ着きます。
Gotokuji ni sugu tsukimasu.

We've started again.
運行が再開した。
Unkou ga saikai shita.

Where are you?
今どこにいますか。
Ima doko ni imasuka.

We're just coming into Shimo-kitazawa.
下北沢に着いたところです。
Shimo-kitazawa ni tsuita tokoro desu.

No, I didn't forget the gifts.
いいえ、プレゼントは忘れていません。
Iie, purezento wa wasurete imasen.

See you at Shinjuku South Exit.
新宿駅南口で会いましょう。
Shinjuku eki minami guchi ni imasu.

What's the name of that izakaya?
どの居酒屋ですか。
Dono Izakaya desuka.

I don't really remember the name.
名前を覚えていません。
Namae wo oboete imasen.

Wait until you see this new phone.
この新しい携帯を見せるね。
Kono atarashii keitai wo miseru ne.

Bye.
またね。
Mata ne.

14

By-line
Setagaya Line

Odakyū, change at Gotokuji. Down Stairs Exit.
Cross-street to Setagaya Line. Yamashita-eki.
Two stops to Shimo-Takaido. ¥140.
Railtrain. Railmap. Railpoem

三軒茶屋	Sangen-Jaya	**Three Teahouses**
西太子堂	Nishi-Taishidō	**West-Taishidō**
若林	Wakabayashi	**Young Woods**
松陰神社前	Shōin-Jinjamae	**Station Before Shōin Shrine**
世田谷	Setagaya	**Seta Valley**
上町	Kamimachi	**Upper Town**
宮の坂	Miyaosaka	**Miyan Slope**
山下	Yamashita	**Below The Hill (TRANSFER ODAKYŪ LINE)**
松原	Matsubara	**Pine Tree Field**
下高井戸	Shimo-Takaido	**Lower Well**

Yamashita-eki
Train-parking

The Setagaya Line gives you a number of sights, small-scale, agreeable, largely those of a well-heeled residential area. Back and forth Yamashita to Shimo-Takaido two especially reach out for notice.

Mid-way is Matsubara-eki. There, to the right side in the direction of Shimo-Takaido), is pinioned on to the back of a house nothing less than a train-carriage façade. Two bumpers. Driver and/or guard-window. Red and cream. Left side signal arm at rest. You look at it one train-to-another, working carriage to retired carriage. Home, the heart, is where the railway is?

The other sight (left side heading towards Shimo-Takaido) gives the promise of relaxation, the body in spiritual harmony with the spirit. Or it almost does. The name of the place wonderfully jars. Massage Factory.

SETAGAYA CORRIDOR

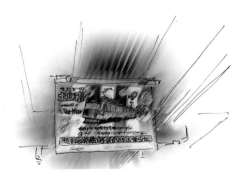

BOROICHI

Twice a year, December and January, there is Setagaya Boroichi, the so-called Rag Market with origins in the sixteenth century. Kind of better-class flea market. Antiques, collectables, eats. Eight hundred or so stalls and a nearly quarter-million browsers and buyers. And situated between the Setagaya and Kamimachi stops on the Setagaya Line. Day-time throngs. Night-time lit by chains of bulbs. Old 78s. Magazines. Posters, Ceramics. Furniture. Coins. Fossils (or fake fossils). Munchies from *niku manjū* (buns made of pork filling) to cotton candy. Old and young foragers. Street buzz. Street cheerfulness. Relaxed market Japan – with the flash and click of photography everywhere. The Setagaya Line two-car trains are never fuller.

Shimo-Takaido Eki
Shimo-Takaido Station

Shimo Takaido
Keio Line
Upstairs
Mall.
Japan
Train Mall

One
Two
Three
Four
Five
Train
Mall

1. FROMENT D'OR. Bakery and Café. Cakes and bread. Drinks. As in all Japanese bakeries select choice by large hygienic tweezers. Then tray. Legend – by-the-door:

   Nous efforçons de communicer (sic) la culture alimentaire française en vous apportant un produit s'attachant a l'art du pain dans sa matiere et sa fabrication

2. YOSHINOYA. All-orange décor beef rice-bowl eatery. Massive popularity. In and out eating.
3. QB: 'JUST CUT HAIR'. ¥1000. Three chairs, two employees, one room.
4. LAWSON STATION. Convenience Store. Onigiri to Newspaper. Drinks to *sembei*. *Konbini* commercial cousins include *7-11, Family Mart, AM/PM, Ministop, Sunkus, Newdays*. And, as the Odakyū's own kiosk cum supplyship – ODAKYU-OX. One of the great fea-

tures of these *konbini* is the *takkyubin* service (the name is actually the trademark of the Yamato Transport Company, a bit like Hoover for vacuum cleaner). A door-to-door national delivery service. Killingly efficient, cheap. You can send most-sized boxes, foodstuffs, books, papers, luggage. Just head for a *Konbini*, sign the delivery form, pay, and your things will reach their destination within 24 hours. Literally *takkyyubin* means 'home delivery post'. Perfect definition. Perfect service.

5. JB BANK. Post Office Bank. *Yūcho Ginkō.* ATMs.

15

March Wednesday

➲

Mid-afternoon journey aboard the **Local**. Standing. I lean forward and, to my astonished eyes, there's Sigourney Weaver battling an extra-planetary serpent. A bit more tactful leaning confirms a student-aged youth wearing fashionable Japanese long-toed winkle-picker shoes absorbed in watching *Alien* on his *keitai*. Just the thing. Double rows of razor teeth. Lethal saliva. Acid blood. Tentacle lashing. *Nosferatu*, more aptly *Godzilla*, next? Maybe a longer journey and he will be watching the whole five (or is it fifty-five) TV series of *24* with Kiefer Sutherland at the helm?

Which brings one on to reading. Today, same journey, I count about seven people book-reading in the carriage. Both seated and standing. The Odakyū as Open University library-branch. When bookstores sell a book they usually give you a book-cover – in part to advertise but also, one has to suspect, in anticipation of train-reading or the like. And this, for fellow-passengers like me, causes a frustration. I can't be alone in wanting to know what's being read – all you see is the brown cover. MARUZEN, KINOKUNIYA, TAKASHIMAYA, REGULUS are typical, not to mention ODAKYŪ BOOKMATES and one simply labelled BOOKS. But what is inside? Sheer none-of-my-business carriage curiosity.

It may or may not be Buddhist writ, a sense of the world appointed as it is and in necessary equipoise. But that does not help the *gaijin* passenger when an empty can starts rolling across the always meticulously clean carriage floor. Its tinny back-and-forth clang with each sway of the train, the clash against a metal seat fitting or even a passenger's foot, brings no corrective action. This is Odakyū Japan as something like train-karmic, the rolling drink-can as the sound of universe. As we head into Kyodo, no passenger will disturb the *comment c'est*. No reach-down. No recycling as it were. However ear-grating. My own instinct is to kick the hell out of the thing or boot it out of the door. Grab it and crunch it. But I want to be the good train guest.

A word on crows. Crossing the Tamagawa (the Tama River) via the new bridge into Noborito you can not help but be struck by both the working-class bird crowd (pigeons, sparrows and their ilk) and by a certain avian aristocracy (black-headed gulls, buntings, egrets). But the winners for me are always the crows. *Karasu*. They perch like black hooded jurors on the train wires. They swoop on all nearby *gomi* (rubbish). Their loud caws might be public morse-code. And from the train window you see them loop and fling like feathered performers in the Cirque du Soleil. Black feather companions. Train companions. Boon companions.

Phantom Odakyū? From time to time there flies past an empty train, carriages unlit, destination unspecified. You see them parked, incognito, not in service, in occasional Odakyū sidings like the one near Kyodo-eki. How to resist this or that imaginative link? Child trains like *Thomas The Tank Engine and Friends* or Tom Hanks's *The Polar Express*. Heavy-hitter train films from the oh so English *Brief Encounter* to the Czech-German *Closely Watched Trains*. Train *cinema noir* like Hitchcock's *Strangers on a Train* or Christie's *Murder on The Orient Express*. Then there is the literary roster. For the young, E. Nesbit's *The Railway Children*. At adult level, Zola's *La Bête Humaine* and, always, Tolstoy's *Anna Karenina*. There is even the local-bred trains of manga-anime, Leiji Matsumoto's intergalactic *Galaxy Express 999*. All of these might be parked on, or off, the Odakyū Line. Train wheels. Train reels.

16

Odakyū Day-out
Sendagi

➲

千駄木

Time for a small literary trip. Odakyū out of Mukōgaoka-yūen down to Yoyogi-Uehara. Change to the Chiyoda Line. And on through first to Nezu-eki, and then, Sendagi-eki.

Ogai Mori, or in transliterated Japanese, Mori Ōgai. Real name was Mori Rintarō (1862-1922). Hugely important Meiji-era notable, a physician who rose to become Surgeon-General of the Japanese Army, a major medical presence sent to Manchuria in the Sino-Japanese (1894) and the Russo-Japanese War (1904–1905). Trained in Confucian classics, and across a four-year stay at various universities in Europe, mainly Germany. Learned both German and Dutch. Above all, an author to rank with Natsume Sōseki. Novels, stories, histories, essays.

In March 1889, he married Akamatsu Toshiko, daughter of an Admiral, and moved into her family house – a house still standing but now maintained as part of the Suigetsu Hotel Ohgaisu (the latter phrase also **Ogai-sou** or Ogai residence/homestead). He there wrote, or began, his classic story *Maihime* (1890), usually translated *The Dancing Girl*, set in Germany and with its ill-starred drama of damaged love. The abandonment of the dancer of the title who carries her child by Toyotarō Ota: he opts to return to Japan without her. The work has lasted. Mori's marriage did not. Less than a year and he and Toshiko-san were divorced. *Ars longa, vita brevis* kind of comes to mind.

Few later works of fiction better confirm Mori's imaginative grace than *Gan* (first published serially in twelve parts 1911-1913) and translated into English as *The Wild Geese*. Lovely, affecting novella of a woman who allows herself to become the mistress of a money-lender in order to help her ailing father but who falls for a medical student, the very object of desire. Around this triangle Mori creates a busy, circumstantial word of late Edo becoming Meiji Japan. For his last two or so decades Mori lived in Sendagi, in a house which served as a salon that included the novelists Natsume Sōseki and Kafu Nagai and the poets Takuboku Ishikawa and Mokichi Saito. That house was demolished, a successor built. But what remains is the original wall with the kanji for **View, Tide, Tower**, an assumed reference to the possibility of being able to see the Tokyo Bay in the distance.

Intriguing to think that within the original residence Mori wrote his way into fame and literary fortune. It reminds of other writer's lairs, their literal but also imaginative workshops. Texts written. Ink used. Thought given word.

Michel de Montaigne: in his near-Bordeaux 'Tour du Château', his tower, amid books, manuscripts and his own thoughts.

Marcel Proust: in his cork-lined and curtained room at 102 Boulevard Haussmann writing *A La Recherche du Temps Perdu*

Herman Melville: in his upstairs study at Arrowhead, Pittsfield, Massachusetts, composing *Moby-Dick* upon his large writing-desk.

George Bernard Shaw: in his movable writing shed at his Ayot St., Lawrence, Hertfordshire house ('Shaw's Corner') where, after 1906, he wrote most of his plays.

Virginia Woolf: inhabiting and writing her '*A Room of One's Own*'.

17

Shimo-Kitazawa

下北沢

OVERHEARD DIALOGUE

(adjusted fare of another kind)

'I'd really like to get into you'
'He said that?'
'Sure, that's exactly what he said'
'You mean he didn't say I'm really into you'
'Not a bit. He said I'd like to *get into* you'
'Literally you mean?'
'Yep. Literally'
'Jesus. What did you say?'
'I said – excuse me, are you talking to me?'
'And?'
'Back he came. He said it again. I'd really like to get into you'

'I hope you told him where to put it'
'Well, not exactly'
'So what did you say?'
'I asked him who he thought he was'
'And he replied?'
'I'm the guy who'd really, really, like to get into you'
'And then what, I asked him'
'I'd like to do it again he said'
'Were you buying things all the time?'
'Well, kind of looking at things. Then looking at him'
'So what did you do?'
'I bought those Madras Lentils and Makhani sauce I told you about'
'And him?'
'I said to him what makes you think you can talk to someone like
that?'
'And he said?'
'You'
'Me, I said?'
'Yeah, he said, you. I saw you looking at the lentils and knew I had
to get into you'
'Just like that?'
'Just like that'
'Well it's a hell of a thing to say to a woman, especially in Tokyo,
I told him'
'He said it'd have been the same in LA'
'But not in Tokyo I said'
'Why not, he said, you're American, he said'

'But you wouldn't say it to a Japanese woman I said'
'She wouldn't speak English he said'
'What if you said it in Japanese I said'?
'What if – he said'?
'So how many times I said have you told a woman that you'd like to *get into* her?'
'Twice, you're the second he said'
'So I guess I should feel second-best I said'
'And him, what did he say?'
'Kind of he came back quick as a flash'
'So what happens now I asked him'?
'Well, you could say yes he said. We could hop on the Odakyū up to Shin Yurigaōka'
'Why there I said'
'I just moved there he said'
'So I asked him from where'
'Kichijoji he said. I'm working in Seijo and it's a better commute he said'
'You didn't think of going to Shin Yurigaōka with him did you?'
'I was wondering'
'So what happened next?'
'I bought some more Chatplate Choley, curry, and some black beans and brown rice'
'Then?'
'Then he said let's go'
'Did you?'
'Did I what?'
'Go to Shin Yurigaōka?'
'So you can get *into* me I said?
'Sure, he said, why not'

'Because it's no way to talk to a woman I said'
'I know, he said'
'Well what did you do'
'Who was the first woman you said it to I asked him?'
'She was working in a language school – she called the police'
'And, then what happened I said'
'They didn't speak English he said'
'You think that's what I'm going to do I said?'
'Not really he said'
'Why not I said'
'You're not the type he said'
'What type do you think I am I asked him'
'The type I'd really like to get into he said'

18

Bicycle!

自転車

**'Bicycle, bicycle,
I want to ride my bicycle…'
Freddie Mercury**
Queen

**'A strange land of bicycles'
Monica Sone,** *Nisei Daughter* **(1953)**

Approach Mukōgaoka-yūen, North or South, and you cannot avoid a whole Japan of parked bicycles. Station plantations of them. Station fields of them. For which you pay your bike-parking ticket and leave until return.

Arriving bikes. Departing bikes. Corridors of bikes.
Rail-track bikes. Under the highway bikes. Off to the stores bikes.
Student bikes. High school bikes.
Male rider with girlfriend seated side-saddle bikes.
Child on two or three-wheeler bikes.
Bikes.
More bikes.
Yet more bikes.

RAVE

How could you not be in favour of Japan as a bike-country: eco-benefits, no carbon footprint (or pedal-print), reduction of road traffic, easy storage, an aid to physical health and fitness.

If you are off shopping, in the immediate case in Mukōgaoka-yūen, then you can carry purchases in either of the two baskets fore and aft.

Given Japan's reputation as a high-price economy, domestic bikes are astonishingly cheap.

Family bike outings, along a large river like the Tamagawa or a small one like that in Mukōgaoka, can be a lift to the spirits. The Tama even has a special riverside pathway (also used by joggers and strollers). Relaxation. Not-on-the-train Japan.

Sometimes en route to or from the station, you catch the sunlight on the bike handles with the effect of a whole sea of metallic shimmer.

One affecting sight is the (usually older) bike-man who collects cans. Time and again you see a bike looking like some outlandish Michelin-tire phenomenon, a bloated Kitty Hawk. Cans in huge sacks being taken to a nook or street recess to be flattened and then cashed in for recycling.

The ward authorities are pretty good about bike-management. Each bike has to be registered with due sticker. Given any illegal bike-parking (and there used to be plenty around Mukōgaoka-yūen station), a truck comes round to collect all offenders. Handlebar to handlebar, wheel to wheel, they are piled up like some vehicle convict-row. And it costs a fair number of yen to reclaim from the city dump-site. In all a bit of bike weed-clearance. Impressive.

Bicycles give off their own aesthetic. Body and machine, balance, motion. Interestingly, and except for racing-bikes, they all are built with a diagonal centre-bar. In my gender-unreconstructed youth these were known as girls bikes, a bike you would never have dreamed of riding unless you wanted the derision of your fellow male-adolescent youth.

RANT

In Japan bikes are ridden on the sidewalk, the pavement. So just as cars threaten bikes, bikes can threaten pedestrians. They are, after all, vehicles. Time and again you have to dodge or swerve as one comes towards, or even more irritatingly, from behind. Three times I have been caught.

Bells. It may be good practice to use them as warnings. But they are used without inhibition. They may not intend offence but time and again you find yourself startled.

Lights. In theory all bikes at night should have lights, the true and trusted dynamo. Not so in reality. As often as not they glide through the darkness like stealth raiders. You either do not see them or they do not see you.

Mukōgaoka-yūen's small river-canal a number of times gets a thrown-in bike visitor. Maybe student drinks-and-pranks, maybe simply dumping, but not infrequently an eyesore lies in the water

– visited only by the brown carp. On one occasion I saw a local duck squatting on the protruding handle-bars. Feathered easy rider.

Mothers (and fathers) frequently deposit infants in the front or back basket. On my imperfect statistics less than half ensure their progeny wear helmets. A spill, a sudden jolt, and the dangers become obvious.

Bikes and *keitai*. Riding one-handed and with mobile phone in the other: it may well be effortless for the rider but you see lives at near-risk at major road crossings. Padding along in all pedestrian innocence, equally, you yourself become yet again vulnerable to a side-swipe.

Why, you have to ask, are there no bike-lanes, as in Holland or Scandinavia? Should not bikes be on the road as against the sidewalk or pavement?

Bike raves. Bike rants.

19

Odakyū Bike Interview – Toda-san

➲

Ohayo gozaimasu
Good morning
O genki desu ka?
How are you?
Hai, genki desu
I am fine
Anata wa?
How are you?
Hai, genki desu
I am fine

Shifting between Japanese and English this is the nearly every-morning exchange with Toda-san, the kindly, engaging employee of the Odakyū Line who looks after the bike space round the corner from the main bike-parking. He speaks not too much more than basic greetings-English, myself, reciprocally, not too much more

than basic greetings-Japanese. His custodial patch is underneath Fuchu-Kaido, the highway that heads upward to a bridge over the train-lines. There he rules, always a truly benign rule, from 5.30 a.m, to 12.30 p.m. every week-day. Blue-overall uniform, beige base-ball cap with a small red cross and 'Road Safety Committee' written in Japanese. Surveillance from his sentry-box. A greeter of patrons, issuer of tickets, manager of parking rows. The pleasantest man alive. In his late sixties. The following translates a February conversation.

How long have you been working for the Odakyū?
Two years.
And before that?
I worked in sales for NEC first in a branch-office in Nagoya and then in the main office in Tokyo.
Then you retired? Is this *arubaito* (part-time work)?
I retired at sixty from the company. But it's not quite *arubaito* – it's *shokutaku* – somewhere between *arubaito* and full-time employment. Necessary to add to my pension.
And you must live near here?
Yes, a few stops west on the Odakyū Line – at Yomiuri. So I use the Ikuta Station.
What do you like to do when you're not working here?
Most of all mountain trekking, photography and music. I sing in a choir – operas and recitals. In 1992, we sang in Carnegie Hall, the

only time I went to America. I also go to concerts all the time in
Tokyo.

And your family?

My wife and three children. My son lives in Mishima, my daughters
in Shizuoka.

You like the bike job here?

Sugoi. Great. It's fun. All kinds of bikes. All kinds of people. Like
you.

20

International Interlude via Narita Airport

➲

成田空港

Home and Away
Flying-out, Flying-in

Odakyū Line to Shinjuku
Change of Platforms

Temporary Station-Repair Directions To All Lines
PLEASE USE ELEVATOR TO GO UP TO THE
UNDERGROUND
CONCOURSE

Shinjuku to Narita
NARITA EXPRESS (NEX)
Shinjuku-Narita
(All seats to be booked)
Platform place
Right carriage
On time

One hour, twenty minutes later
NARITA AIRPORT

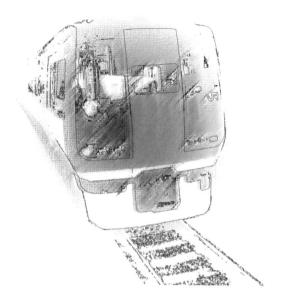

TRAIN FLIGHT

AIR FLIGHT

AIRPORT

South Wing
North Wing
Baggage pre-delivery offices
Leave your coat and collect it on return office
Counter

AIR SEAT

Watch safety video
Seat Belts
Trays in upright position

Baggage stowed
Switch off electronic devices
Taxi-ing

AIRLINE MAGAZINE READING
ITEMS FOR EVERY HOME

Solar Power Mole repeller – works day and night
Life-size Chimpanzee Bust – 'alive'. Latest in Hollywood animal-tronics
Pet staircase – 'designed for pets to 100lbs'. Skid resistant
Advanced large-capacity feline drinking fountain – 'reduces the risk of urinary tract infection and kidney disease'. Bowl and reservoir are dishwasher safe
Hydro Foil Water Scooter. 17 mph.
Fungal Nail Relief 'developed and tested by a leading university'
Bunion Sling
World-Class Pogo Jumpers
The Million Germ Eliminating Toothbrush Sanitizer
Brondell Swash High Tech Toilet Seat
Basho crouches in his mawashi. Cast in quality resin.

DUTY FREE

BE NICE OR LEAVE HANGING PENDANT
DIESEL MALE PERFUME: EVEL FOR LIFE
DAISY (Vera Wang). EUPHORIA (Calvin Klein). BIO PERFORMANCE ADVANCED SUPER REVITALIZER CREAM (Shiseido). SHIMMER BLACK EYE PALETTE (Bobbi Brown), LASTING LIPS (Clinique). ABSOLUTE SEDUCTION PALETTE (Lancôme). SKIN CAVIAR CREAM (La Prairie). CUBA NECKLACE (Antica Murissima). GREY GOOSE VODKA

ALL NIPPON AIRLINES (ANA)
SEAT INSTRUCTIONS FOR FIXING TABLE

Stow and latch controller for Taxi, Take Off and Landing

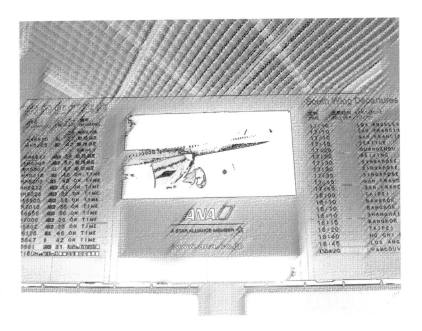

NARITA RETURN

YŌKOSO!
WELCOME!

The end of the walk is ahead. Please watch your step.

HEALTH CHECKS

This is the Health Consultation Room. If you have any health problems such as fever or diarrhoea please drop by the health consultation room.

MINISTRY OF HEALTH, LABOUR & WELFARE
QUARANTINE SERVICE
(Please use Yellow form)

It is generally known that there are many kind of serious infectious diseases abroad, which have not occurred in Japan. Even if you contracted such a disease, you wouldn't show any symptoms when entering Japan because of the incubation period.

If you developed any symptoms such as fever, rash, abnormal bleeding, diarrhoea, and jaundice within 28 days after arriving in Japan, you should consult a physician as soon as possible with showing this card.
Quarantine Station

NARITA PASSENGER NOTICE

TERMINAL DIAGRAMS

Re-Entry Permit Check
Retina photograph
Two finger-print photograph
Passport stamp
Disembarkation Card for Re-entrant
Baggage

NARITA EXPRESS
(or 'Friendly Airport Limousine' – i.e. Bus – to Shinjuku)

21

Keitai Train Culture

➲

To be without a *keitai* in Japan, and certainly on the Odakyū, is to be caught cybernetically nude. A train-aberration. They inhabit every bag, pocket and chain. They hang from straps-around-the-neck. They poke out from handbags. They are manufactured in a rainbow of colours, Shinjuku salaryman utility-black to Harajuku teen-girl pink. Their ring-tones can be alarm clocks or musical.

Japan is nothing if not a culture of icons. Temples. Shrines. Advertising. Satchels. Restaurants. When the Cui-dore (Kuidaore) restaurant in Osaka closed in 2008 after sixty years of business nearly the whole of Kansai (and beyond) headed into grief-therapy. Not because of the food, good as it was reputed to be, but because of *Cui-dore Tarou*, the bespectacled full-sized mascot clad in red and white striped clown suit. This was prime time news, front page newspaper reportage. It might have been better reported in the Obituary columns.

The Japanese *keitai* might be another fetish-of-fetishes. The young, especially, have them be-decked in mascots (*masukotto*), charms, tassels, chains, a whole variety of talisman.

One day to the next, and from your Odakyū perch, you see mobiles with their *sutorappu* – silver medallions, intricate chains, a satin puff-ball bit of décor, different types of bead, multi-colour threads, actual

and fake keys, small crucifixes (Japan is about 2% Christian), finger-rings, snippets of lace, even bottle-openers. Small soft-toy dolls or dogs or bears come into play. Hearts in plastic or metal (sometimes with arrows slanted through them) figure prominently. Occasionally

there is an *omamori*, a temple good-luck charm. This is truly to engage in your own *keitai* shrine decoration. How not to think it homage to telephonic gods, the presiding deities of speak-to and be spoken-to? A religion of *keitai*-ism? Telephonism?

   And then there are keitai on the move. Train colloquia. Getting off the train colloquia. Striding forth colloquia.

   Plain old-fashioned, non-stop natter. Odakyū natter.

odakyu

22

April Thursday

⮕

World War II. Europe. Between Chitose-Funabashi and Kyodo. That is, I am seated on the **Semi–Express** and, standing with his back to me is a middle-aged man wearing a leather 'Bomber' jacket engraved with a detailed map of the Normandy invasion. Omaha Beach. Utah Beach. Gold Beach. Juno Beach. Sword Beach. German and Allied battle lines. The American Airborne Division. The Pointe-du-Hoc German fortification. All of it in golden-colour pencil as though some displaced brass rubbing. Oddest feeling to be on a Japanese train in 2008 watching a piece of train garmentry, a jacket lay-out of the war. Makes me wonder if you would ever see on the Paris, London or New York metro a coat-map of the Japanese invasion of Manchuria. The man in question, however, innocently, quite passenger-ly, holds on to his carriage strap.

Aha! Big Day in Mukōgaoka-yūen eki. The new lifts or elevators have been installed. Slow, stately up-and-down beasts, a mere one floor level up from street level, and both South and North. For weeks there have been the ubiquitous blue tarpaulin covers, hard-hat work-men and supervisors, and truck-loads of equipment. Eventually, all Odakyū stations, where necessary, will have lifts. This one may have come early because the Romance Car stops at the station. Whichever the reason the upshot is convenience time for the elderly, for moth-ers with push-chairs, for parcel-carriers, and for myself whenever there is a suitcase to be lugged into Shinjuku. Lime-green frame. Also see-through glass, so even if you are not travelling in the lift, you can see the looped cables, the wheels, the intricate engineering. Odakyū engineering.

Two schoolgirls get on at Seijo, maybe twelve or thirteen years old, in sailor-girl uniform. Both have in hand their flicker-lists. With a bit of careful craning of the neck I can see they are doing ENG-LISH VOCABULARY. Each mouths a word, checks the Japanese for it, and then flicks on to the next word-ticket. It is as though they are using carriage mini-dictionaries. Two assiduous lexico-trainees. *Eigo ichi* (first-year English).

Three schoolboys this time. Boisterous (well, Japanese-boisterous). Duly done up in Prussian-style school uniforms, yet with a necessary semi-punk accoutrement. Pants, in accord with teenage-boy writ, hang massively down, with boxer-short elastic waistbands in view. Both are eating *tai-yaki*, fish-shaped confectionary filled with sweet bean paste. The smell is pungent, sugared. An older lady, positioned in the PRIORITY SEATING (*yūsenseki*), looks at them thunderously. Pure age-marinated outrage. Not *her* Japan, not anything her generation's girlhood would have done. Just eating on the train should be enough to bring down the dragon gods. Train sacrilege. However clean, orderly, the Odakyū, for her at least, this threatens a Fallen Estate.

Jinshin jiko. 'Personal accident'. Literally 'human body accident'. Such is to be heard over the Odakyū and other intercoms from time to time in connection with a train delay. Put bluntly it means someone has jumped. A train suicide. For all its well-being, the evident general post-war affluence, Japan has an estimated 30,000 suicides a year, roughly 2500 a month, 600 a week. Death on the tracks or at the level-crossing is part of it. Quick and certain immolation. But no small trauma also for the train-driver or station personnel. In September 2009, there was the latest suicide at Mukōgaoka-yūen. The resulting train delay would seem to have been the least of it.

23

Odakyū Tamagawa

RIVER RUNS

TRAIN BRIDGE

You are out for a stroll, river-side. Take a glance in the direction of the bridge. Back and forth pelt the Odakyū trains. **Expresses** and **Locals** in their cream-and-blues. **Romance cars** each in their identifying colours.

CAR BRIDGE

A VIEW FROM THE BRIDGE

You are crossing the newly widened rail-bridge between Noborito-eki and Izumi-Tamagawa-eki. To the north and south flows, or rather half-flows, the Tama river. The *Tamagawa*. Heartening sight. A wide stretch of running water to irrigate, and confound, the square upright geometry of the bankside residence-blocks. Odakyū trains become viewing-platforms, box-seats, mobile verandas. Geographers will confirm that the Tamagawa begins high in Yamanashi Prefecture, heads into Lake Okutama and then winds across the Kanto Plain via Noborito and elsewhere until it spills into the Tokyo Bay.

Its up-country runs are familiar kayak and canoe hang-outs. Bikes can be hired to ride its banks. Flora and fauna buffs walk its surrounds. It holds a fond place in many a Japanese and Tokyo day-out memory. Childhood walks. Swimming. Outdoor lunches. Plain messing-about.

FLOOD BARRIER

Placid as for the most part the Tamagawa seems, it can rile up on occasion, especially in Tokyo typhoon weather. To that end a barrier has been built. Like rivers throughout Japan the Tamagawa is thus

subject to the concrete treatment (annually Japan uses more concrete than the USA). In a way you favour the barrier if indeed it is a life-saver, a hedge against serious flood. On the other hand it takes on the look of river genetic engineering, a species of surgery against nature. No doubt it has to be, but a pity.

A BEND IN THE RIVER

The river itself, plus reeds, birds, the flip of a small fish, light eddies and currents, all make a perfect counter to the trains. Their rhythm and sound are given perspective. The water as ever in Japan serves as respite, a tranquility.

BAIT AND TACKLE

'Look at the crowds of water-gazers there'.
                    Herman Melville, *Moby-Dick*

What more congenial sight as you speed this way or that aboard the Odakyū than the Spring-to-Autumn, dawn-to-dusk, local fishermen out (or even not especially out?) to make a catch. At peak there are

crowds of them, happily seated or standing, fishing lines extended out, at ease. Likely retirees. The river is always fairly shallow so you have to wonder if the fish do not somehow swim sideways up. Or that they do not know that a thousand hook-concealing worms tempt only to trap. Either way it is *The Compleat Angler* time, Izaak Walton transported from seventeenth-century England to twenty-first-century Japan.

24

Station Sights

KITAMI EKI

Gaze through a window in the platform back wall (Shinjuku direction) and there is a plaque advertising a wondrous private clinic. Namely **Brain Treatment System**. Couple of visits should have you thinking more clearly.

KYODO EKI

Nothing like a good dental ad. Not least as you gaze from the Kyodo platform to a wall poster calling you to **Sarurai Dentalpia**. Could be a tooth-convention, even a deviant tooth-tendency.

SANGUBASHI EKI

Couple of stops from Shinjuku and there is an invitation to step into time as much as place. A platform sign reads – '**Please get off at this station for Meiji Jingu**'. The original shrine was built to commemorate Emperor Meiji and Empress Shōken, destroyed in World

War II bombing, and then re-created in 1958. Historic modernity
several times over.

MINAMI SHINJUKU EKI

Essential facilities. Clearest word-and-picture indication, men and
women, of where to go when you have got to go.

SETAGAYA-DAITA

One of several temporary plastic wall-coverings as the Odakyū-sen
engineering work proceeds. Full of tile-like pattern. Small blocks

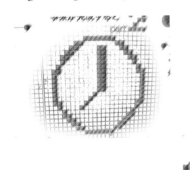

colour-squares. With a small effort of imagination it puts you in mind of Mondrian or Miro. Japanese station cubism with a dash of Europe?

SWITCH TO GINZA LINE
LET'S KIOSK, WHY NOT?

Newspapers
Sweets/Candy
Pens
Cigarettes
Magazines
Knick Knacks

25

Odakyū-sen
Yoyogi-Hachiman Eki

⊃

Alight at Yoyogi-Hachiman station going east into Shinjuku and two platform posters (and spelling) do their trick:

BODDY HERRBS – MASSAGE
www. boddyherb.com

FORMOSA – TEA HOUSE

RESTIA MANSIONS
ODAKYŪ REAL ESTATE

YOYOGI HACHIMAN
SHRINE

Entrance
Steps
Torii

Entrance Steps

The shrine itself is estimated to have been built in 1212 in the name of the fighting god Hachiman.

Yoyogi Hatchiman Shrine

Temple side-road Torii

Yoyogi-Hachiman Bridge
Yoyogi-Hachiman

Vietnamese Embassy – Signing

Vietnamese Embassy – Roadside view

26

May Friday

Day in, day out you get on the train at Mukōgaoka-yūen. But only this Friday did I notice the outside sign on the local 'personal hygiene' emporium. A store selling shampoos and hand-soap, toothpaste and make-up, house-cleaning tackle and medicines. The sign, however, reads WEL PARK. Having consulted the local street directory, I find it belongs to a drug-store chain called Welcia Kanto Company. Even so, the urge is now on me to spiderman up the wall and add what to my own eye is a missing 'L'. Thoughts of L-shaped rooms flood in, not to say long-ago school geometry lessons and those squares and oblongs measurement exercises.

Rooftop vistas. Setagaya Daita and Soshigaya-Okura. Both have yet more 'mansions', moderate high-rises at once shoeboxes and in tiers, and with balconies of reach-out-and-touch train proximity. How do people living inside them manage – passing train noise, the near presence of huge metal transportation within arm's length of where your head may be resting? Then there is the laundry. Pegged and hanging out for immediate passing inspections are shirts, sheets, undies, an array of towels. Rail-track dormitory. Odakyū life-cubicles.

Today I found myself sitting opposite a male passenger, not so much a salaryman as a sports jacket and cords type. I was just about settling in for my vertical read of *The Japan Times* when, like some junkie readying for his fix, he rolled up his left sleeve and with his right hand reached into bag for…a pair of tweezers. Without a by-your-leave he then started tweezering out hairs from his arm and on it went for some time. Not something to make you feel good about breakfast. And there was a whole other arm to go. But then an unusual bit of drama. An older woman, breaking with all rules of non-interference, gender status, and seated on my side of the carriage, suddenly shouted at him – 'not here, not here'. Startled he got his tweezers back into the bag, rolled down his sleeve, and virtually jumped out at the next station. Quite a thing.

MEAT advertising. For a Japanese culture at once fish and rice or tofu and sushi centred, it is more than a nice paradox that the Oda-kyū carries two eye-catching sets of American meat publicity. One is for the ubiquitous McDonalds – the NEW DOUBLE QUAR-TER POUNDER. With the accompanying phrase BIG MOUTH. The Japanese gloss says none of these things. There is also a pointer to Fries and Coke. Wonderfully at odds, discrepant, not least in a Japan that uses chopsticks. The other, no doubt to make up for the scare about US beef and BSE/Mad Cow Disease, extols the virtues of American beef. Two images, posted on the carriage wall, give respectively a pastoral or farm vista of grazing cattle and a benign cowboy with child in hand, the other a green field and a kindly-custodial farmer. Beneath which reads **www.americanmeat.jp**. Carnivore Japan?

The Odakyū has a new hanging-strap policy. At one end of car-riages there is now a series not in white as usual but YELLOW. These, we are led to believe, are where all phones should be switched off – a quiet zone. In fact, even as passengers sway to the carriage's rhythm, the odd ring-tone is to be heard, the odd '*Moshi, moshi*' ('Hello'). A Japan almost anywhere without the *keitai* would be a virtual impossibility. Yellow straps look good. They give a change of colour. But they are up against the might, the beckoning electronic ease, of Docomo, Softbank, AU, and all their fellow nationwide communication companies.

27

Mukōgaoka-yūen Day for Night
(With a Nod to Truffaut)
Day Sounds, Night Sounds

DAYTIME

1. 9.30 a.m. Jingle-music for the rubbish collection. *Gomi* (rubbish). *Gomi*-collection. Blue and white truck.

SCHEDULE IN JAPANESE AND ENGLISH

Ordinary Waste – Tuesday, Thursday, Saturday
Empty Cans, Pet Bottles, Empty Bottles, Used Batteries – Monday
Small Metal Articles – First and Third Tuesday

Oversized Waste – Please aplly (sic) with Oversized Waste Center
(sic) Kawasaki City TAMA Waste Collection Office

2. Blaring loud-speaker perched atop a white truck. Said truck
    moves with agonizing slowness so the 'broadcast' hovers in the
    ear. Morning and afternoon. Scrap metal collection.

    Sodaigomi kaishūsha desu ('Any scrap? Lots of scrap?') *Tĕpurekōdā*
    (tape-recorder). *Terebi* (TV). *Pasokon* (personal computer). *Rajikase*
    (radio cassette).

3. Afternoon. *Gyōza!* Small van with endless looped recordings.
    Dumplings Galore. Finger-sized. Scalloped edges. Flour base.
    Ground pork and cabbage filling. *Nira* (vegetable) or leek or
    onion. Garlic. Ginger. Sake. Soy sauce. Sesame Oil. Dipping soy
    sauce. Echo of ancient street-vendor.

4. Evening. *Tofu.* No voice. Simply a cornet or horn. Tradi-
    tional. Infinitely recognizable chords. Seller on motorcycle with
    wooden box of *tofu* on back.

5. As in every Japanese city, town and village, and almost as though an anthem, there is to be heard the paddle-beating of futons. The futons are hung over the balcony, or over one of the laundry poles fixed to the balcony bracket, or simply over a clothesline. Whichever the case you hear the rhythmic slap, the one after another expulsion of dust or tics as the paddle goes about business. From the street it often sounds like you are being followed. Footsteps.

NIGHT-TIME

1. Semi-surreal encounter. Walking home in seriously dark nighttime when, suddenly, out of nowhere pops up this metallic voice. Droid intonation. Straight out of *Star Wars* – C-3PO. I had not fully realized that I was walking past a TALKING DRINKS VENDING MACHINE. Extra small lights flash, then *Irasshaimase* ('Welcome'), and a menu follows:

    O-nomimono (drinks), *jyusu* (juice)
    mineraru wō-tā (mineral water), *kohī* (coffee)
    aisu kōhī (iced coffee), *o-cha* (tea)

The whole is rounded out with a *domo-arigatō zaimasu* and a small anime-like manikin-girl bowing. Pure electronic other-world.

Maybe a version of Dr. Who's Tardis? Or an illuminated monolith out of the Stanley Kubrick/Arthur C. Clarke space-epic **2001**? Is that what those black rectangular plinths are — inter-planetary drink-machines? Not to mention HAL. And Japanese-made? Miraculously no more than a week later, the machine disappeared. Likely it has been teleported to some as yet un-named terra-forming planet. Or just maybe to a hospital as a high-tech defibrillator, maybe as one of the play-units in a Games Centre.

2.   Second semi-surreal encounter. Another seriously dark night-time. And a yet other voice from nowhere. But, not unreasonably or unnaturally, speaking Japanese.

Ima kaeru tokoro
I'm on my way home

Doko nano?
Where are you?

Konbini no soba
Near the convenience store

Jitensha?
Are you on your bike?

Un
Yes

Kaimono tanonde ii?
Can you get me something?

Nani?
What?

Mentsuyu. Onegai
A bottle of *tsuyu*

Wakatta
OK

Jāne
Bye

Yes, it is a silent bike-rider of disembodied voice. No lights. Pedal-
ling so slow you can not hear anything. Phantom-cycle. The mind
wanders. Hamlet's Ghost. *When We Dead Awaken.* One hand on
handlebars. Other hand with *keitai* to ear. And it is girl to mother.
Bit of a further come-down, however, when you know that *tsuyu*
is a type of dipping soy sauce for soba noodles. And that the *konbini*
round the corner is a SUNKUS, one of hundreds in Japan. So much
for the Bard. So much for Ibsen. All too real-world terrestrial. Just
off the Odakyū-sen and would you pick something up from the store
for me. Errand-time.

28

Odakyū Day-out, Hakone

➡

箱根

HAKONE

National Park just over a train-hour due south of Tokyo. So, first, a morning **Express** from Mukōgaoka-yūen to Machida. And from there, with booked seats on the Odakyū Line's finest, it is the Romance Car all the way. Any one of these bullet-nosed beauties will do, each colour-coded, each logarithm'd so to speak – the 7000 (LSE), 10,000 (HiSE), 20,000 (RSE), 30,000 (EXE), 50,000 (VSE) or 60,000 (MSE). Presumably the 40,000 somehow went missing in action? As to Hakone itself it holds near-mythic properties for Tokyo-ites and the like, a kind of Japanese Lake District, local Dordogne or Yellowstone. You get there after maybe a *sembei* (rice-cracker) or two, an *onigiri*, and a swill of *o-cha* (green tea). Even an early *eki-bento*. And then it is Mother Nature. Tree-lined hills, greenery, challeng-ingly clean air, valleys and groves. A spot of ex-volcano, or at least its impact, is to be had at Owakudani and other mountains–and–valleys. And if you are thinking of nights-over, then it is the *ryokan* (Japan's traditional inns with *tatami*-mat and futon room and exquisite dinner – *kaisaki* – and breakfast) and the infinite pleasures of the *onsen* (hot springs with the obligatory small towel for modesty purposes). Edo Japan. Vintage Japan.

HAKONE WEST

But we, this time, are headed for the Hakone Open Air Museum. From Hakone-Yumoto it is on to a red connector-train which does switchbacks to get you up into the mountains. Positively Swiss. Bird-life. Lakes. Sightseers. And then, after disembarkation at

Chokoku-no-Mori, the museum itself. Spacious viewer pathways. Small Appian Ways of busts and profiles, both ground-level and aerial sculpture. Colours, materials, forms and compositions spread out against the sky. You cannot help but feel a touch oceanic, spatial. And in the company of some of the world's best. One centrepiece has to be the 300 Picassos, cubist and other canvases to fish-engraved plates, at the duly named Picasso Pavilion. Another is the world's most extensive Henry Moore collection, gloriously rounded figures in motion and at rest. But you are also in the company of Rodin and Miró and relative contemporaries like Marta Pan (*Floating Sculpture*, 1969) and Gabriel Loire (*Symphonic Sculpture*, 1975). It is the human hand set down amid Nature's hand. Lovely interplay. Open air interplay.

Amid this plenty, comes 'Miss Black Power' (1968). One of the many huge female forms created by Niki de Saint Phalle (1930-2002). Her name, you get tempted to think, maybe a tease by Nabokov. Not so, of course. A bit of biographical digging tells you that she was born in Neuilly-Sur-Seine, took early to painting, moved with her family to the States, became a fashion model, and married Harry Matthews, Old Princetonian and later the author of baroque, post-modern-to-a-fault fictions like *Oulipo Compendium* (1998) and *My Life in C.I.A.* (2005). There was a breakdown, a move back to Paris, the influence of Gaudí and Dalí, and her run of titanic doll-like women-sculptures. She would marry the Swiss sculptor Jean Tinguely. Later came her NANAS series and the TAROT GARDEN in Tuscany. And here she is, in Hakone, represented by this iconic black woman.

Black head. Squared shoulders. Body big as Africa. Miró-like dress – painted blue veins or lace. Breasts like circle-painted targets. Blue handbag. Two black legs the thickness of Egyptian pillars. There she stands. Monumental. Black gynocentric strength. Do not mess with me. This is *our* time, *our* 1960s. And against a background of dulcet Hakone trees and shrubs. A black anywhere woman. A black everywhere woman. A black here-and-now and in-Japan woman. IN YOUR FACE.

In Your Face

HAKONE EAST

Over hill and dale time. Endlessly round-the-mountains bus from Hakone to Lake Ashi. *Ashinoko*. A journey of road curve after road curve, glimpses into gorges. And then, 30-40 minutes on, one last downhill and you are in the small port of Hakone-machi. Water's edge. Another volcano-crater fed by mountain streams and rivulets. And as you look out an exquisite picture seizes the eye. There, as always stately, and this time snow-tipped, is Fuji-san. Japan's gift from the gods. Nature's own sculpture. And within Nature's own frame at once mountain-white, water-blue and shoreline-green. The lake itself is placid, given to gentle ripples, shimmers of light. In the distance, incongruously to a fault, there is one of the several replica pirate-ships to lure tourists, keep the children happy. To your right is the green-tree'd promontory and, positioned exactly in front of it, and in the lapping water, is a perfect red-painted *TORII*.

A pointer to the *jinja* or shrine behind it, exquisite and yet but one of the estimated 80,000 throughout Japan. It could not be more Japan. For this is Shinto. The marker between sacred and profane. The entrance into holy-spiritual space. No matter that there are other *Torii* everywhere – at the shrines of past emperors, at a thousand temples, even as an icon at the US's 101st Japan-based Airborne Division with its World War II to recent Afghanistan history.

This *Torii* is held perfectly in place. A red geometry of spirit. Totemic. At once liminal and yet wholly precise. You get your own western-eyed glimpse into *wa* as a term, a concept, derived from the Chinese *wŏ*. Peace, harmony, balance, grace. One of the oldest *kanji* in existence. The *Torii* acts as a focus, a drawing-in point for all the Nature about it. Even the water at its base seems to do homage. To be sure you can move on to the shrine-complex (*shaden*), the bells and rituals, the stone stairways and ceremonial halls. You can remind yourself of Shinto festivals and worship (*matsuri*) at the changing of the seasons. But here at the edge resides the necessary moment, the natural *haiku*. Wherever the Odakyū Line has taken you in Japan it has rarely delivered better than this.

29

June Saturday

➲

En route to Mukōgaoka-yūen, walking along the road one tier down from the arterial main road, or *dori* (Fuchu-Kaido), that runs parallel and also crosses over the Odakyū rail-track. Cross-over bridge steps just ahead. There suddenly heaves into view a truck carrying a section of aircraft fusillage. Square passenger windows. Nose-cone. Wing fixtures. Something of a rare, certainly unexpected, sight. But it fits perfectly into an Odakyū travel-frame – foot passenger, train, track, bicycle (as stored under Fuchu Kaido) and plane. A day later some kind of refrigeration-truck comes with the words 'Fixed temperature circulation system of the highest refreshment'. Quite.

Cám o'n. The Vietnamese for 'Thank You' would not necessarily first come to mind in connection with the Odakyū. But a visit to the Vietnamese Consulate in Yoyogi-Hachiman for a brief trip to Ho Chi Minh City led to overhearing the phrase at the station. Which, in turn, connects to other overheard bits of Odakyū foreign language. Hellos mainly. *Nih hao* from a group of Chinese students. *Sawasdee* from a Thai businessman. *Namaste* from a Nepali chef (in white-smock embroidered with cooking pot). Once a Frenchman asked 'C'est la ligne Chuo?' 'Non, Monsieur', I came back, proprietary to a fault, 'C'est la ligne Odakyū'. *Ma ligne* I might have added. Tokyo, however international in an evident sense, is actually not quite as international as New York, London or Paris. But it is a great city in which to be international.

Midday **Express** to Shinjuku, spot of shopping, then on to the Keio Line bound for Shimo-Takaido. Train pauses at Sasazuka-eki and, like a team of green-clad and bandanna'd foragers, there board the poster-men. Eight no less. They dismantle all hanging posters and clip on their successors (from huge mail-bags) at the speed of nano-robots. New posters flicked into straightness, lofted, fixed, and occasionally lightly slapped like new-born infants to test viability. Down carriage. Up carriage. Next carriage. The posters themselves bring into view new kanji, new images, new commercial eye-fluff. Kind of pre-industrial assembly line. Pure dispatch.

Rooftop vistas. Near Kitami-eki. Roof-garden, summer-green square. Plants and flowers. Nothing unusual in that *per se*. But amid the lego-like 'manshons' (so-called), the assembly-by-numbers residential blocks, it hits the eye like welcome news, Nature's own singing telegram. Kyodo, like so many other Odakyū stations, is latticed by overhead wires. Cable-webs. Telegraph poles to right and left like some electronic forest. A near-Tokyo full of pulse-arteries, sound-veins. Electricity. Energy. Hum. Nearer still to Shinjuku, between Minami-Shinjuku and Shinjuku, you see from the Odakyū window, just about, the Tokyo Metropolitan Government Building. One of Tokyo's tallest. Narrowing triangle office windows. Skyward. Perpendicular Japan.

ODAKYŪ VOICE. Under this label the Line has introduced wall-posters and station-posters full of smiling platform personnel. White gloves, arm-rings for rank, immaculate dark uniforms. They seem to incarnate service. Inquiries fielded. Umbrellas returned. The disabled given help. All good fare. But it has to be said that their Yamanote Line brethren do this on electronic wall panels, together with interactive news headlines, commercials, route-maps, and station announcements. The Chuo Line even plays an anime-*manga* serial 'My Darling is a Gaijin' (*Darling wa Gaikokujin*), the funny-barbed portrait of a European-Japanese marriage by Saori Oguri first published in 2002. The Odakyū will surely follow.

30

Odakyū Commercials

➲

Carriage and Platform

SUBARU – FANTASTIC MOMENTS

MICRO-DIET – SUNNY HEALTH

SHOUT DIET. SMILE DIET (Beer)

CHIKAWA STATION (New Station) – GRAND OPEN

KIRIN SPARKLING HOP

JAPANESE GOVERNMENT BONDS

KIRIN BEER – STRONG SEVEN, 7% ALCOHOL

TOKYO NÚMERO (Men's suits)

PIANISSIMO FRAM – FOR WOMEN (Cigarettes)

L'ESPRIT SANTE ET PHYSIQUE (Massage)

PACHINKO AND SLOT

ASAHI BEER STYLE FREE

DAIHATSU – INNOVATION FOR TOMORROW

BOSS COFFEE RAINBOW – SUNTORY

NTT COMMUNICATIONS – 'CreativE-Life' for Everyone

BLACK CAT (Yamato Transport) – MOVE YOUR TOMORROW

ORA-2 (toothpaste) – STAIN FREE

NOLOAN.COM – NO LOAN BANK

SHINSEI BANK – COLOR YOUR LIFE

FRISK (peppermints) – SHARPENS YOU UP

31

Odakyū Smokes

➲

Like Spain, Greece, China, or much of Eastern Europe, Japan is a smoking country. Of late, however, prohibitions have begun to bite. Trains were required to be cigarette-free some time ago. Workplaces and restaurants are slowly following suit, but by no means all. Cigarette machines are everywhere, not least in or near stations – even if you now have to prove by means of a card that you are over twenty to buy. The Odakyū is no exception. These dispensers, scaled down tobacco-warehouses as it were, come framed in electronic lights and instructions. Insert. Press. Collect. At the same time, in carriages and on stations, the No Smoking signs proliferate. A war

of inhalation. A war of exhalation. A decade ago smokers using the Odakyū were asked to stand in white half-circles on the platform, so that you saw them puffing and exhaling smoke like groups of Roman conspirators about to fell Caesar. Smoking remains a challenge in Japan: the engrained cultural reflex not to interfere with others, the eco-wish to be smoke free.

ENGLISH-LABELLED BRANDS

2009 Prices – ¥500, ¥320, ¥300, ¥180

Mild Seven	Aster
Seven Stars	Hi-Lite
Aqua	Lark
Cabin	Marlboro
Kool	Kent
Next	Caster
Bevel	Cherry
Hard	Parliament
Camel	Marlborough

Salem   Carleton
Icene   Hope
Cabin   Noire
Lucky Strike   Alaska Menthol

LADY-BRANDS

Pianissimo   Lucia
Bevel   Lark Mild
                     Virginia Slims

32

By-line,
Nambu Line

南武線

KAWASAKI CITY

From Mukōgaoka-yūen one stop by Local on the Odakyū Line to Noborito-eki. '*Noborito desu.* The next stop is Noborito.'

NOBORITO STATION

'Please transfer for the Nambu Line'

Down the speaking escalator to the **Nambu Line** platform. Said
escalator leaves no doubt. In self-reiterating Japanese it announces:
'This is the Escalator down for the Exit. Don't stand at the beginning
or end of the escalator. Please stand inside the yellow lines.' All good
notification as it were. Useful, I imagine, for sight-impaired passengers. I myself listen, look admiringly, and obey.

Nambu Line, then, and all stations to the city of Kawasaki.
Names are a bit confusing here – Kawasaki-shi is normally translated
as Kawasaki City. But that covers the whole region or province.
Ourselves are headed to the city itself, very much a shop-and-
residence conurbation created since the war. And for a two-point
visit: **sludge** and **peace**.

First a Nambu stop-by-stop ride to Kawasaki-eki, but not without a moment at the station before Kawasaki – the orthographically
challenged Shitte (blessedly pronounced Shi-tay).

Exit Kawasaki-eki and on to a Number 10 bus bound for the out-
skirts. Our mission: to visit nothing less than the **Iriesaki Composite
Sludge Centre**. There, even as the mind thinks waste pipes and

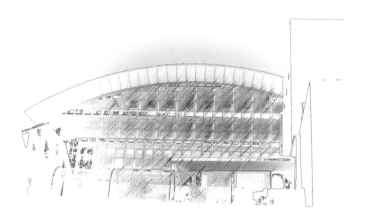

sewage farms, dark intestinal processes and vents, one encounters the **Iriesaki Heated Swimming Pool.** Children to be seen swimming. Special rates for seniors.

All in the one complex. It is a radiant conjunction, sludge, huge metal transformers, water reclamation, pool lanes, kids, pensioners. Another view adds some of the metal construction.

Back on the trusty Number 10 bus to Kawasaki and a half-dozen stops up the Nambu Line and it is time for The Kawasaki Peace Museum and Park, the latter in romaji the **Kawasaki Heiwa Koen**. Alight at

Musashi-Kosugi-eki, ten minute walk and there is the Museum building. **KAWASAKI PEACE HALL**. So inscribed in Japanese.

And then the park, a grassy knoll or patch. Various stone sculptures, notably **War and Peace** by the American artist Jim Sanborn. Together with companion pieces.

CIRCLE

UPRIGHT

JUNCTION

33

Odakyū Bag Watch

➜

World Wide Love – Red paper carrier bag
Mysty Woman – White paper with black string handles
Armani-Ginza Tower – Black shiny paper bag
Love Drug Store/LDS – White and orange plastic
Sportiff – White carrier bag
Hey, The Medium Dreamed – Standard Journal – Brown paper
Mono Comme Ça, A Simple Lifestyle Are What We Suggest
– White/black canvas
Authent – Shiny black plastic
Fareg, Scappe Uomo – Pleated black paper
Freak's store – Brown canvas
Womb – Green plastic
Tokyo College of Music – Grey canvas with blue stripes
Né-Net – Plain brown
Winter Party Diamond – Red cloth with gold letters
Snoopy Studios – Black canvas
Mochi Cream – White and grey paper
Mars – Zebra striped bag with pink string handles
No Music, No Life, Tower records – Small yellow bag
Pornograffiti – Blue plastic
Death – Black leather sports bag
Super Hakka – White paper carrier bag
Liz-Lisa – Lilac paper bag
Espace-Hiroko-Koshino – White plasticised paper
Scapa – Brown with dark-brown string handles
Spirited – Pink cloth bag
Brownie bee… – Black paper with red lettering
Afternoon Tea – Brown plastic in yellow and blue capital letters
Spinns – White and purple plastic
Ingni – White plastic
Café do Brasil (é um producto da athletica. s.a) – Black bag
with arm-strap
Milk – Black canvas

Jeanasis – Black paper
Lowry's Farm – Blue plaid bag
Tama Plaza 20 – Tawny Canvas bag, blue lettering
Silent Lumy – Green plastic
Kaldi Coffee Farm – Orange-brown paper
Optical 88 – Black paper, white letters
Emily Temple Cute – Red and white square paisley, plastic
Daydream – High gloss white
George's Christmas – White and red (plus holly) paper
Comme Ça ism – White paper
Naked – White paper, red lettering
Napoli – Purple gloss
Ego – Black and yellow plastic
Quoi? Quoi? – Light purple paper
Santa Crée Hair Make Team – Black and white plastic
Omnibus Japan – White Plastic

34

Seijo Times

➲

Seijo has become something of a stellar station, still only two plat-forms but double-tracked on either side. It has a newly minted Mall, four levels. Why? It does not, after all, have interconnecting Lines. There is a university but that would not quite do it. There is the Kurosawa/Toho Studios connection. But the real reason, one has to suspect, is that this is prime Tokyo turf. Prime real-estate.

Seijo exists at the southern edge of Tōkyo-tō – the tō signify-ing metropolis, right at the border with Kanagawa-ken where Mukōgaoka-yūen and all stations on to Machida and beyond belong.

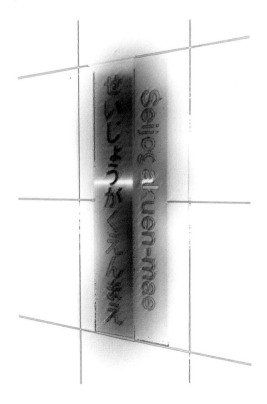

It is full of high-price mansions, veritable trophy housing. So maybe the station has been be-malled to suit. Whatever the explanation it now has a whole phalanx of restaurants, clothes shops, knick-knack places and up-market groceries.

MALL

Four levels. Enter by the street and you have a comprehensive wall-warning: 'No Smoking, No Open Flame, No Dangerous Goods.' You also have the Organic Café Gris ('Green Innocence Organic') and the Albion Café ('Precious Coffee Moments'). To the ground-level 1F South there is a Starbucks, a *kōban*, a Trois Gros bakery. To 1F North you have the Hôtel de Suzuki for fruits and the Pharmacy Nira. Head up the escalator and one upon another gallery opens to you. 2F has the Hansel and Gretel clothes shop, plus an Italian-style restaurant called Elévé. At 3F and you have access to the Gaba, the English Language School, and Asta Aveda, the toiletries and hairdressing salon. Reach 4F and you are literally at a ceiling of restaurants. *Tempura* and *soba* Japanese. Slow Chinese Food (so-called). Another Italian restaurant. A French-style restaurant.

The whole amounts to Seijo as tiered shop and eat parade. A silhouette of Tokyo. With Odakyū trains ever-ready.

STEP OUTSIDE TO TOWN LEFT. EARLY MORNING

STEP OUTSIDE TO TOWN RIGHT. EARLY EVENING

And in a nice flourish
Seijo
Mall
gives
you
a
rooftop
olive
tree
garden
with
restaurants
to hand

Eating in
Eating out

Different
menus

SEIJO TRAIN TIMETABLE

This is something of an electronic beauty. It not only gives all arriving and departing trains as expected. It alternates Japanese with English and in colour-coded interactive design. Worth staring at for itself and never mind the trains.

CHECKING IN

CHECKING OUT

35

Odakyū Day-out, Yokohama

横浜

JAPANESE YOKOHAMA

It is the Odakyū first to Machida, and from there via the Yokohama Line, to Ishikawachō Station. Best foot forward for five to ten minutes to the waterfront and Yamashita Park. There, near hotel and restaurant lined roads, you have a vista worthy of Japan's second largest city, three million and still growing.

The eye cannot but oblige with a full panoramic round. The Ocean itself and upon it whole sea-lanes of shipping, cargo-vessels to fishing-boats, coastal ferries to small leisure-craft. The Yokohama Bay Bridge, metallic, car-busy. Two towers – the Landmark Tower (one of the tallest buildings in Japan) and the Marine Tower (a lighthouse kin to the Eiffel). A great Amusement Wheel. At nighttime the carnival of lights. The water's edge also looks to the *Hikawa Maru*, stationed full time and sedately after plowing its way cross-Pacific to Vancouver and Seattle and back from 1930 to 1960. A tribute to early luxury ocean cruising but also a hospital ship during the war. Weekend and day-out strollers. Children. Hawkers. Music. Dog-lovers. Bird-cries.

History? Step back to Commodore Perry's landing at nearby Uraga in 1853 and the opening of Japan, or to the Great Kanto Earthquake of 1923 which nearly destroyed Yokohama, or to the US Air Force B-29 carpet bombing of the city in 1945 and Japanese surrender. Museums? A choice of the manuscripts at the Kanagawa Museum of Modern Literature, the manikins of the Doll Museum, the patterns and textures of the Silk Museum, or the alimentary riches of the Soba Museum. Sport? You could go to the Yokohama Stadium, built in 1978 and home of baseball's Yokohama Bay Stars, or the Yokohama International Stadium, built in 1998 and host to soccer's 2002 FIFA World Cup Final (Brazil 2, Germany 0).

But like all great ports Yokohama has its human mix and match, a migrant face. It may well have been a yet further forward-marker that the first English language newspaper, the *Japan Herald*, was launched in Yokohama in 1861. Or that it had the early twenti-eth-century Foreign Settlement area (called the Bund as in Shanghai) prior to the Kanto Earthquake. After the earthquake there were also the vigilante killings of Korean and Chinese as if they had taken advantage of the disaster. Pluses and minuses. Losses and gains.

For whatever else, Yokohama yields key signs of nationalities that have added width and depth to Japan's own. A challenge to usual asser-tions of all-of-a-kind cultural homogeneity. An enlarging of apan.

AMERICAN YOKOHAMA

Impossible not to think General Douglas MacArthur. His role is well enough known, America's own *shōgun*, the re-maker of a Peace

Constitution Japan under its Emperor. He also requisitioned most of Yokohama. Nowhere does the city more carry this America than the waterfront Hotel New Grand. Except, maybe, and on a lighter note at historic jazz club-land like the *Chigusa* and the *Mocambo*, or at the Honmaku Jazz Festival begun in 1981 and the Yokohama Jazz Parade begun in 1993. Designed by Watanabe Hitoshi, opened in 1927, a model of art deco modernism yet with a Japanese precision of line and space, Hotel New Grand still vaunts an Admiral Perry Room and – to be sure – it was MacArthur's first Occupation HQ. Make a visit there today and you may well have to work hard to reach back to this history. An eighteen-storey tower was built in 1991, high-rise hostelry. A one-time photography shelf of the Occupation has gone. The hotel hosts wedding bazaars. Yet beyond this updating and refurbishment the imagination has good reason to remember the early US and other trader-clans, and indeed the Kanto earthquake catastrophe which led to its being built, the World War II bombings, the General's corncob pipe, and the post-war Japan rising out of defeat. It is a hotel to reflect both Japan and America, their conjoined time past (and yet time ongoing) not simply witnessed but sedimented into its very bricks and structure.

CHINESE YOKOHAMA

Yokohama may not be entirely synonymous with the sight and sound of its Chinese-heritaged population, but it comes close. *Yokohama*

Chūkagai. Yokohama Chinatown. The largest in Asia. Enter by the lavish red and gold Friendship Gate (*zenrin-mon*) or by the East and two other compass-point Gates.

Over two hundred restaurants and almost as many groceries. Head for the Kuang Di Miao Temple, built to honour the god of prosperity and business.

Venture into Daska, the nine-storey theme store, created in imitation of Shanghai. Dragon and flower festivals. At night a lantern and neon city. History again rises from the streets. This is the Chinese Yokohama begun from 1859 and the opening of Japan to free trade. This is the Yokohama of largely Cantonese settlement and the staging-ground for Sun Yat-sen's revolutionary movement against the Manchus in the 1890s. This is the Yokohama that caught the tidal brunt of the Sino-Japanese War in 1937. This is the Yokohama in which tourism has replaced portside sailor bars and brothels. A day-out? You eat, wander, and remember yet another Japan-history. China's Japan.

FRENCH YOKOHAMA

With the demise of Les Halles in 1969, Paris's hallowed covered market with its meat, fruit, vegetables and all associated produce, and the transfer to Rungis in 1973, bids were put in for the cast-iron frames. One came to Yokohama with the result that a stroll down the waterfront will bring you to within sight, and perhaps memorial sound and smell, of that market. The metal uprights and roofs call up other-side-of-the-world France, an emblem for the many French-style *brasseries* in Yokohama, in Tokyo, and in the Japan beyond both. At the same time might it not almost be an Isamu Noguchi sculpture-installation, Japanese geometry in its own right?

INDIAN YOKOHAMA

Yokohama has long had a population from the sub-continent, Merchants, seamen, latterly restaurateurs. Plumb centre of Yamashita Park, a hail from the sea, stands the Indian Drinking Fountain.

The inscription reads 'The Drinking Fountain Presented to the City of Yokohama in Memory of our Countrymen Lost in Earthquake, September 1923'. Erected in 1965. Four Pillars. Verdigris dome. No matter that the fountain does not actually have water: this is a solemn tribute to a significant segment of a population also lost to Nature's convulsion. Japan and India have myriad connections, not least the Buddha, trade, foodways, even the Sanskrit on different shrines. Here, in smaller scale, is another.

MULTINATIONAL YOKOHAMA

Other Yokohama is everywhere to hand – Brazilian, Filipino, Tamil, Australian, British. But where better, or even more oddly, to recognize something of the migrant variety of Yokohama than the Foreign Cemetery (*Yokohama gaikokujin bochi*)? Established in 1859. Nearly 5000 graves. For the most part American and European. World War I memorials. US and British Memorials. A French section. Crosses. Occasional Stars of David. A hillside of burials. A hillside of overseas lives lived in Yokohama. Nothing if not multi-Yokohama. And all of it under the ever observant eyes of those gossipy-cawing local crows. Avian multiculturalists every one of them...

36

July Sunday

➲

Air conditioning. The Odakyū has two levels. Soft and Normal. The second carriage from the front, the second carriage from the back. So you have to make the big decision – step from outdoor heat-humidity into cold or moderately cold air conditioning. Either way it can be welcome. But also a sure-and-certain route into summer colds. Round the clock sniffing, sniffling. And it is not done to blow your nose in public. In theory, the sniffing, the sniffling, has to be delicate. In fact there are some pretty big sniffs, not to say sniffles.

Cool Biz. Under the LDP government regime of Prime Minister Junichiro Koizumi (2001-2006) and 'to fight global warming' men were urged to forego ties and pitch for the open-necked shirt and short sleeves. This was the Koizumi of Post Office Privatization, Koizumi the aficionado of Elvis and Wagner. Salarymen thus abandoned years of sartorial practice, be-knottedness. 'Special' open-necked shirts were advertised. Those still reluctant to forego old habits kept their ties but stylized their loosening – tie-pin in place with the tie a good 100+ millimetres open and at an angle. Just as Koizumi's ample, winged hair (for which, and his politics, he became known as 'Lionheart'), became his personal insignia, so his espousal of men's cool-biz shirts remains one of his legacies. Visible daily aboard the summer Odakyū Line.

Full Odakyū Apache. The phrase echoes Takayuki Tatsumi's *Full Metal Apache: Transactions Between Cyperpunk Japan and Avant-Pop America* (2006) with its wide-ranging take on East-West cultural inter-image. It comes to mind during today's **Express** trip from Mukōgaoka-yūen to Machida. Normally you see salarymen in regulation black, grey or blue suits, or uniformed school-goers (Prussian-military for boys, sailor-style for girls), or a range of normally kitted other commuters. But today, maybe because it is Summer and a Sunday, a sight of rainbow exuberance. Student-aged woman. Yellow shoes. White inset sock. Tights with different-coloured spiral pattern. White frilly skirt. Russet jacket. Tee-shirt top with a yellow fish floating against a black background and emblazoned with the word **ELSE**. White ear plugs and foot tapping. A whiff of André Breton. A whiff of Female Pied Piper. Great mix and match. So much for Odakyū conservative dress codes.

Another sweet sight. Groups of old people heading out for the likes of Hakone or Lake Ashi. Walking groups seated aboard the train. What you notice is the greatly purposive apparel – men's bandannas, ladies's small, floppy plant-pot hats, kerchiefs, plus small backpacks, walking sticks, right boots. And the sheer gregariousness. Japan as aging society at its most cheerful. A June Odakyū outing. Just the thing. Little wonder that Taro Aso, then incoming LDP Prime Minister in 2008, known as Gaffe Central and by chance his own name a perhaps English-language pointer, hit a deepest nerve when he said of a population where more than one in five is over their mid-sixties 'Why should I pay tax for people who do nothing but eat and loll about drinking?' Obviously quite off the rails. He needs more than a few outings himself on the Odakyū Line.

Vignette. Odakyū Girl 2008. Teenager. Dressed in eye-catching shades of white. White, almost spectral tube-dress. White boots with black zig-zag stripes. White braided-wool rose in her hair. Above all blond-dyed hair and white-string headband. Pure Jazz Age. Dancing Odakyū. Flapper Odakyū.

37

Odakyū Trains of Thought

➲

Travelling the Odakyū-sen, almost inevitably, spurs association with prior train travel, runs of past time and change.

Journey upon journey you give way to lost-in-your-seat meanderings. Or by the window recollections. Odakyū memory chamber.

MANCHESTER-VICTORIA TO BURY ELECTRIC TRAIN

The English 1950s. Yours truly in teens (11-18 years). Seven years, thus, of home to school to home. Word reaches me that this old-fashioned, clanking, separate-carriage train, with its third rail, has now yielded to a multi-hinged modern trolley. But the station names, some of them improbably arcadian, have been retained – Bowker Vale, Heaton Park, Prestwich, Besses o' the Barn (which gave its name to a celebrated North-of–England brass band), White-field, Radcliffe, Bury. The school itself an old-style and work-horse

English Grammar School. Entry by 11+. O Levels and A Levels. Aboard the train there was late homework, a first bow into French, Spanish and Latin. School blazers had the obligatory tag of Latin – *Sto ut serviam* – pseudo-chivalric but not quite the thing as you grew up close to fading textile and coal Lancashire with its silenced factories and un-smoking chimneys. Almost worthily pretentious. Memory summons a Welsh bantam-rooster of a woodwork teacher whose unwitting signature phrase was 'Right boys, stand by your vices'. The appointment of a High Anglican headmaster led on to the singing of Monday morning religious services in which we were enjoined to Lift Up Our Eyes to Heaven – which we did one week to see some fellow-miscreant had written 'Fuck Off' in reverse mirror-writing in the dirtied skylight. It was a school actually built around 1912 in utilitarian red-brick but in an earlier incarnation, some miles away, had been attended by the aristo who became Lord Clive of India. A connection vaunted by the municipal powers-that-were at every turn. Apparently he was expelled. For some obscure reason we were forbidden to go to the station during the lunchtimes, always a temptation as it had a rare snack-machine. A time when you actually bought tickets from the ticket office. Was it school or school train-journeys with those platform and carriage boy-antics where you weathered adolescence?

NORTHERN LINE, LONDON UNDERGROUND

First half of the 1960s. London undergraduate/postgraduate studies. I had 'hurried on down' in the title-phrase of John Wain's 1953 'angry young man' novel. The Northern boy stepping into London

as Soft South. The capital, transformingly, was nothing of the kind.
A tough, a-buzz, welcome metropolis. A city eye-opener. Trafal-
gar Square and Oxford Street. Parliament and the Albert Hall. Soho
and The Marlborough pub. Early into betrayal of Manchester roots
– university, theatre, politics (or its student version), even a first ballet,
a first opera. And Dillons and Foyles and up to Hampstead for second-
hand books. And where better to get ferried to each than aboard that
old dog of a track the Northern Line (to veterans the Misery Line)?
Goodge Street. Warren Street. Backwards and forwards to student
flats in Kentish Town and Tufnell Park through Camden Town. You
could still smoke on the Tubes, so it was travel by asphyxiation. Occasional Northern Line forays south of the river, the Oval or the seeming near South Pacific of Clapham Common and Tooting Bec. I seem
to have read whole shelves of Penguin Books, seated or standing. Plus
the *Evening Standard* which had a crossword I could just about manage
(even staying on to Highgate once to get it finished – and even then
I had it wrong). Northern Line stoppages were virtually a way of life.
'Signal failure', a phrase to ponder, and 'work on the line', made for
familiar announcements. You became a Londoner by Underground.
There was also growing change-of-line savvy. Central Line. Circle
and District Lines (with 'mind the gap' at Victoria). By post-graduate
time it was on to a thesis on American literature, on Melville. Wholly
unusual choice for a Beowulf-to-Virginia Woolf 'Eng. Lit.' student,
not to say from within a department that was full of Randolph Quirk
grammar (one of my undergraduate years I shared a flat with the lin-
guistics magician David Crystal). So it was the White Whale on the
black-marked Northern Line. And it pointed less to a station-change
than a sea-change, to America.

US RAIL-TRACK, PRINCETON-UNION STATION NYC

First American academic year – with no less than a dozen to follow
at intervals. Departure as Fulbrighter from Southampton on the
old *Queen Elizabeth*, a ship, as I then thought, bigger than Siberia.
I remember feeling I had to somehow match this grandeur, and took
Thomas Mann's *The Magic Mountain* with me. So while Hans Castorp
was dealing with his TB and a world about to fissure into 1914–18 in
his Davos sanitarium in the Swiss alps I was merely getting sea-sick
in the Atlantic. But New York, then Princeton, made for recovery.
Manhattan as Modernism's own city. Princeton as Ivy League-WASP
redoubt. And, to be sure, there were the train journeys between
both. First the Little Shunter (The Dinky), so called, from near the

university to Princeton Junction. Then a kind of veteran workhouse Express, through Newark, with glimpses of northern New Jersey's industrial mess. Yellow-fetid chemical smoke. Rutherford and thoughts of William Carlos Williams and Allen Ginsberg. Into Manhattan along tracks that went into tunnels beneath the Hudson and street-level. Fabled Penn Station, inspired by Roman Baths and the Brandenburg Gate then only recently and controversially renovated from its modernist hey-day of baronial Waiting Hall, colonnades and caryatids. And there, seen for my own first time, the Empire State and fellow needle skyscrapers, the numbered Avenues and Streets. A city to be grasped, learned. Staten Island Ferry with its 25-minutes-ride past the islanded Statue of Liberty and the New York and New Jersey shorelines. The Bowery. Wall Street and the financial district before the Minoru Yamasaki architected World Trade Center Towers. Greenwich Village. Central Park. Upper West and Upper East Manhattan. Even an Anglo-glimpse into the Harlem of 125th Street. Chinatown and city Spanish. And by a train into its very bowels. What more could have suited? What better railway turn-style? NEW YORK, NEW YORK.

BRITISH RAIL, CANTERBURY EAST-VICTORIA STATION

UK University Lecturer. Near three decades, on and off, of British Rail southeast train travel. From Chaucer's medieval Canterbury to Dr Johnson's 'when a man is tired of London he is tired of life' metropolis. As functional a Diesel-and-coaches as could be, through Dickens's Chatham and Rochester, across the Medway, then on to iconic-suburban Bromley South, and into Victoria – accorded its own Tube Line in 1968 (with an extension to Brixton in 1971). Initial encounters meant ear-hurting slam doors and delays announced to be caused by 'leaves on the line' or 'trouble with the points'. One of the busiest commuter tracks in the country, so always best caution to travel, if possible, off-peak. The authorities then made the decision to move the last train out of Victoria for Canterbury East from something like 11.40 p.m. to something like 11.10 p.m. The upshot was that if you were doing the town it was hell-for-leather-time by bus or Tube to Victoria. Theatre finales were now at risk. Shakespeare's Act Vs, Pinter's *The Caretaker* with its tramp-hero off to Sidcup to 'get his papers', Christie's *The Mousetrap* and all who-dunnits. Likewise closing Opera arias, *Aida* to *Tosca* ('Excuse me, very sorry, sorry again, last train'). Even a late fish dinner could have you skipping dessert, impatient to get the bill. But the defining

feature of those days, and well into the 1990s, was the phenomenon of 'the rear four coaches'. The train divided at Faversham, the
rear-coaches hooking up with another train that took you to seaside
Whitstable and from which, if you were Canterbury-bound at 1 a.m.
of a Winter's night, there seemed NO RETURN. The rest of the
train headed on to Dover via Canterbury East. Were you seated four
or five coaches from the rear (no through-passage between carriages).
Had you dozed past Faversham? A slip of train mathematics and you
were the doomed captain of the *Flying Dutchman*, the 'Wanderer' of
British Rail's own Old English poem – with a Day Return Ticket
all to no avail.

PAOLI LINE, 30th STREET PHILADELPHIA

Pennsylvania. Visiting Lecturer year at Bryn Mawr College, 1971–
72. Welsh-Quaker place and station names along Philadelphia's Main
Line. Narbeth. Ardmore. Haverford. St. Davids. Berwin. Bryn Mawr
itself. One of them, Merion, always reminded me of Clough William
Ellis's Welsh folly, the Hotel Portmeiron, where the 1960s TV classic
series *The Prisoner* was filmed – with its penny-farthing logo and
Patrick McGoohan as Number 6 and his clipped 'Be seeing you.' As
you got off and on amid all that affluent colonial-stone housing you
half-expected to hear the occasional 'Bore da', Welsh for 'Hello.' But
nothing like was to be heard and the train headed to Paoli, named in
honour of the nineteenth-century Corsican freedom-fighter General
Pasquale di Paoli. Unexpected overlap of Wales and Italy. Another
pièce de résistance lay in the 30th Street Station, portal to Philadelphia
as City of Brotherly Love and which you reached with glimpses of
the Schuylkill River. There was the Art Deco waiting-hall, now I
see called a 'lounge', walled with monumental figures and the bronze
memorial to Penn Railway employees killed in WW II. After my
own time the station would supply settings for films like Peter Weir's
Witness (1985) and M. Night Shyamalan's *Unbreakable* (2000). Philadelphia, bought by William Penn from the Lenape people, gave
you Independence Hall and the cracked Liberty Bell, Rittenhouse
Square, Market Street, and Chestnut Hill, along with the Museum
of Art (now replete with its outdoor statue of Stallone's 'Rocky')
and streets of Row Houses. Frank Rizzo, ex-Police Commissioner
(dubbed 'the cop who would be king') became the bruiser-mayor.
In one panel of memory, a bitter December morning, I was standing on the Ardmore platform. The only other person in view was a
20 year-old or so pacing with cold and impatience. Suddenly, from

nowhere as it seemed, he put his hands to his mouth, and yelled into the rail-track permafrost 'COME ON TRAIN, GODDAMIT'. My own of-that-moment Paoli Line sentiments to a tee.

CHICAGO L – EVANSTON

Chicago. 1970s-80s. Visiting Professorships to Northwestern University in Evanston. To head by train into Chicago, the Windy City, from just north of the city line meant the 'L', Elevated. Overhead through suburb, then into the North Side, with the rock-lined and jogging-path Lake Michigan shoreline just about in view. The arterial Halsted Street North meant Wrigley Field (home of the Cubs), the Cabrini-Green estate and gay-centred Boystown. Halsted Street South meant a route into Hyde Park, the remaindered Stockyards and black Chicago – Harold Washington would become the first African American mayor (1983-1987). One of my own key friendships was with the novelist Leon Forrest, begetter of the longest black-written novel ever, *Divine Days*, which tells Chicago as though it were biblical-apocalyptic. Back-and-forths on the 'L' were mainly to the Newberry Library, with its vast Melville and Native American Culture collections. But to get there was something of a dance. First the transition from Summer-humid sprinklered lawns to street city – offices, liquor stores, residential homes, high-rises, eventually The Drake Hotel and Playboy Club. Then there was the Newberry in Washington Square Park, a nice patch of greenery amid the Chicago blocks. At the time, however, it was also a druggie hang-out, dealers by the railings. So you could step on an occasional sidewalk, or pavement, syringe even as you made your way into the pages of America's classic sea-writer. Maybe such was somehow signalled in the fact that the 'L' has to be one of the screechiest lines in existence, high-decibel to a fault and nowhere more so than on the swerves. On another trip, to the South Side, one of the remaining white faces as we headed past 56th Street and the University of Chicago, I once saw a winter's broken-down train marooned as it were. It had iced over like some sculpted metal refrigerator-cube. Plus wind-chill. Hog Butcher for the World it may have been in Carl Sandburg's poem. But here, high on the 'L', it was Chicago as frozen chops. Sub-zero boxed meat.

TALGO MURCIA-MADRID

Spousal family-base in SE Spain. Murcia-province. Murcia-capital. To get to Madrid means first *la estación*, Murcia del Carmen, and thence four or so hours north and inland aboard the TALGO – *Tren Articulado Ligero Goicoechea Oriol*. Nothing less. And bound for Madrid-Charmartín. All of it under the rail-banner of RENFE – *Red Nacional de los Ferrocarriles Españoles*. Key passed-by or stopped-at station names read like figures out of a Cervantes text or a Pedro Almodóvar movie. Alcantarilla, Cieza, Hellín, Albacete, Villarobledo, Alcāzar de San Juan. Chamartín you'd call smart-modern, arcades, a moviehouse. As against Madrid-Atocha, named for Our Lady of Atocha (a parish and also a galleon sunk off the Florida keys in 1622) with its palm-tree atrium and the site of the 2004 bombings. Neither station is more than a Picasso's *Guernica*, well a Metro stop, away from the Reina Sofía Museum. Murcia-Madrid vistas en route include Quixote-style windmills, and that brown-shrub landscape indicative of an ever dehydrating country. It is also a train that delivers some of the best eats. Even basic sandwiches. *Jamón y queso*. *Tortilla*. *Chorizo*. Plus *cerveza* or *vino tinto*. *Patatas fritas*. And, to be sure, *agua* (*con gas o sin gas*). But the memory of a one trip especially fixes itself in the mind. TV. The train used to have a TV set bracketed in every carriage. You had no choice but to watch, or shade your eyes, or listen. The movie that day was none other than the sumptuously kitsch *Anaconda*. So there you were, munching on one of the aforesaid *bocadillos* when, Up the Amazon, looms a 40-foot animatronic snake. Slitherings. Writhings. Under-river and even up and down a waterfall. Then, coup de grace, swallowing Jon Voight, white hunter, whole. Not to say regurgitating him cocoon-like later. Quite put you off your sandwich. But the TALGO got in right on time. New Spain.

CALIFORNIA AMTRACK

Several-times-over Visiting Professorships at Berkeley include steps down the coast to friends at San Marcos, an hour or so drive from San Diego. Then visits from there back up the coast to just south of Santa Barbara. Amtrack round-trips from Oceanside Station to Ventura Station, via Los Angeles Station. West Coast sun. The Pacific. Fruit, greens, sunflowers, picking. Jack London or John Steinbeck, kind of, not to mention Jack Kerouac, by rail. You do not always think of the coastal West as train-country, despite the Hollywood-version robberies of Jesse James or Butch Cassidy ('this is a hold-up'). No doubt the upshot of America's 'first love-affair', the car, from Henry Ford's Model T to GM's SUV. But there it is – AMTRACK. Losing big money yet kept in play by Congress and the State. More good station names. Long Beach, Lompoc, Irvine, Fullerton, Oxnard.

A sense of Native, Spanish and Anglo settlement embedded in each. You cannot but note the sheer number not so much of suitcase foot-passengers but of bikes and their Gary Trudeau/Doonesbury helmeted owners. Old-fashioned conductors with tickets wedged in their caps. Not the fastest train but a compensation in watching the sea edge alternate with the farm fields. In the one sweep bobbing surfers, cream-laden sunbathers, and pastel seafront houses. In the other sweep lettuce, peppers, melons, patchworks of green growing things. A thought arises as the train works its way towards La Ciudad de San Francisco…if you could swim west a merest 5000 miles, you would reach Yokohama with Hawai'i for mid-ocean rest and recuperation. Then a quick smack of the SUICA, a hop along the Yokohama Line to Machida, and you could transfer back on the Odakyū Line. **Local** or **Express.** Either one would deposit you back at Mukōgaoka-yūen. Trains West. Trains East. In rail-imagination England and Spain, America and Japan.

38

Train Signs, Train Sounds

DOOR SIGNS

CORRIDOR SIGNS

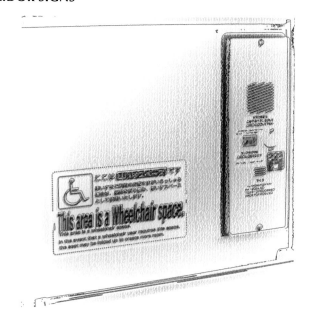

REQUEST SIGNS

EMERGENCY SIGNS

NO SMOKING SIGNS

MORE PLEASE SIGNS ('MANNER SIGNS' IN JAPANESE)

Please do not make a commotion on the train (fight scene)

> **Please do it at home** (woman applying make-up)

Please do it in the yard (man with umbrella practising golf swing)

> **Please do it in the pub** (man with beer-mug in hand)

Please do it at home (youth eating pot noodles)

> **Please offer courtesy seats when needed by others** (two young men on phones – passenger with broken leg standing)

Please yield to each other when passing through

39

By-line,
Tama Express

KAORI MURAJI'S SPAIN

Music time. Classical guitar time. An evening concert by the infinitely talented Kaori Muraji with the New Japan Philharmonic Orchestra.

But, first, trains. Mukōgaoka-yūen to Shin-Yurigaoka and a change there to the **Tama Express** bound for Odakyū-Tama Centre. By repute this was concrete suburbia, a grey city outpost 20 kms from Central Tokyo. So in the 1970s the powers invented Tama New Town (*Tama Nyūtaun*), a 200,000 population 'housing development'

served by three intersecting Lines – the Odakyū Tama, the Keio Sagamihara and the overhead Tama Toshi Monorail.

So what holds? Nothing if not glorious oddity. First has to be names. The centrepiece is the Greek-named Tama Sentah Parutenon (*Tama Centre Parthenon*), a pathway (Parutenon ōdori) through mall-like stores and shops rising upwards towards the galleried culture-complex. A kind of would-be Champs Elysée main artery. Only not. Actually far from it.

First it is out of the station and into the street. Follow the signs.

Then it is eyes left and right and follow more signs.

Parutnenon-ōdori leads on to a run of sub-Elysian steps, if not a stairway to heaven then to the bit of greenery beyond.

To be sure there is the Concert Hall. But there is also, off to the left, the SANRIO PUROLAN, a games and show-time fantasy playground for children and dedicated to the cult anime-cartoon cats KITTY and DANIEL. You enter via a *Stargate*-style arch with Disneyland turreted walls to both sides.

Flocks of infants go there with their flocks of parents. Not cheap. On 2009 prices, ¥7300 per adult, ¥2000 per child, under 4s. free. Infinite adoration and gazing. Kitty parades. Kitty performances. Kitty photo booths. Store-shelves of HELLO KITTY doll sales.

The Centre also holds other jewels. The Living Faith United Methodist Church which also offers free English and Chinese classes. A huge Mitsukoshi Department Store. A 'green' business complex (the CSK Centre). A Warner-Mycal Cineplex. Under the rail-tracks a free-trade zone had emerged. A swap-meet.

Plus due eateries and every manner of small shop.

PLUS THE ART CENTRE

And it is to there, and into the company of the good Muraji-san, that we are bound.

First her on-stage arrival and bow. A frequent Japanese competition winner she began learning guitar at three years of age. Won the Idemitsu Award in 1995. Not to mention four Grand Prix Prizes. Trained in Paris at the Ecole Normale de Musique, returning to Japan in 1999. A regular on NHK and with the Japan Philharmonic. CDs. The film *Contrastes*.

Slight, engaging, impeccably black-gowned, she is preceded by a performance of Haydn's Symphony No. 70 (1779). Four movements under the conductor's baton of Christian Armink, one-time assistant

to Seiji Ozawa and current director of the New Japan Philharmonic, who himself looks young as a Viennese teenager.

And then Joaquín Rodrigo's 1939 'Concierto de Aranjuez'. Three movements this time, *Allegro con spirito*, *Adagio* and *Allegro gentile*. Lovely. Spain's Royal Palace of Aranjuez given score and performance by both composer and instrumentalist. It occurs to you how very right it would be if Muraji-san were to play in performances of all Spanish music. Later you find that this is music recorded also by Miles Davis, skated to by Michelle Kwan, and played of all places in an episode of the BBC's *Fawlty Towers*.

Finally Francisco Tárrega's 'Recuerdos de la Alhambra' ('Memories of the Alhambra'). Exquisite fretwork. Rhythm and cadence. The guitar as world. Muraji-san as world. Spain as Japan. *España como Japón.*

And where more unlikely than in a concert-hall round the corner from an emporium in which HELLO KITTY holds sway? And all reachable by the Odakyū.

40

August Monday

➲

There is nothing if not a language-poetry to the Odakyū station-signs, especially at larger stops like Yoyogi-Uehara, Noborito and Machida. The names themselves exude a winning phonetics, a syllabic *bonne bouche*. Yoyogi-Uehara does perfect duty with two signs, one for the Odakyū Line, the other for the Chiyoda Line. The former is oblong, white in background, and with an Odakyū blue line running through it. The name is given in Japanese (kanji and kana), in English (or more accurately *romaji*) AND in Korean. It tells you that one station back is Higashi-Kitazawa, and the station ahead Yoyogi-Hachiman. Its Chiyoda-Line cousin, alongside and in parallel, has the Chiyoda green line running through it, its own three-language name, and Higashi-Kitazawa and Yoyogi-kōen given as respectively previous and next stations. Train semantics in small. Design in multiples. Place-names in best clarity and colour. The perfect rebuke to an outsider who thinks Tokyo, Japan, 'impenetrable'.

Today's **Express** trip has me sitting next to a salaryman who, reaching into his plastic bag, brings out a dozen or so CDs, each in its see-through plastic case. He then produces a handkerchief and, like some demented night-cleaner, starts polishing the cases. Furiously. Non-stop between Seijo and Shinjuku. You reach for a touch of Freud or thoughts of the anal-compulsive. But it does not really hit the mark. There he is, almost an Odakyū diamond-polisher, the Odakyū guardsman-marine-commuter doing his parade boots. Each CD and case he holds to the light for artisan inspection. Then, all goes back into the plastic bag and off he marches. The man with the cleanest CD collection in Tokyo.

Education Odakyū. Amid the profusion of posters for electronics, clothes, trips, this or that deal (with plenty of swimsuit shots and proffered limbs and cleavages in view), there are panels advertising High Schools and universities (some with relevant Odakyū station indicated). The universities, mainly private, come over as Pick Your Own academic fruit-and-vegetables – Seijo, Meiji, Senshu, Obirin, Tama, Nihon, Kanagawa, Tokai. Each has its picture of a beckoning

Gate or Building. And assiduous, books-under-arm students. Japan vaunts 600-plus colleges, good to bad, high-tech to finishing school, with *Todai* (University of Tokyo) as Oxbridge or Ivy League pinnacle. Along with The Open University (*Hōsō Daigaku*). Makes you think of Odakyū trains as Faculties and Departments, a rail-track campus.

Nails. Or rather nail-paring. Middle-aged fellow boards at Noborito replete with plain white carrier bag. No sooner has the train lurched off than he produces a pair of nail-clippers (the kind in which you hear the cut) and methodically begins to snip. Finger nail. Thumb nail. One after another. The clippings themselves he deposits in his bag. The whole two hands then done, back into the bag also go the clippers. He does a small inspection of his digital handiwork and exits at Umegaoka. Not a single passenger blinks or reacts, save for a few eye glances. Odakyū on-line carriage discretion in the face of off-beat manicure.

Disney. The lure of Chiba's Disneyland may be legendary. But today, at Setagaya-Daita, a young woman boards with wheeled, hard-shell suitcase. Covered in faux newspaper cuttings. MICKEY MOUSE AMAZES GOOFY. KITTEN STUCK IN TREE – MICKEY SAVES THE DAY. Disney'd Odakyū. Rumour is to be heard that Emperor Hirohito died with a Mickey-watch strapped to his wrist. Disney'd Japan.

41

Odakyū Day-out, Chiba

➡

千葉

Resident Chiba-ites may not thank you for saying so but the region has acquired its modern reputation for two principal reasons: it acts as dormitory Tokyo and it is host to Narita Airport. For sure this does an injustice. Chiba Prefecture *(Chiba-ken)* has any number of other claims. Six million people make their home there, by no means all commuters. If there is industry (chemicals, coal, steel) there is also farmland (rice, *daikon* and other vegetables, flowers), if fisheries (a considerable shoreline extending into the Pacific and Tokyo Bay) then also the Kanto Plain. Chiba was also an ancient hemp-growing region. A 'day-out' can also get you to rivers like the winningly named Mama River or Chiba port, also much beach. Beckoning climate – not least the summer cool.

Two trips in one. Two species of temple visit. First to Narita (properly *Narita-shi*), not the airport but the village, an area known as Sanrizuka. Then to the Tokyo Disney Resort.

Sacred and Secular. Fudōmyōō (deity) and Mickey Mouse (celebrity). The Japan of Indian-imported spiritual tradition, the Japan of American-imported funfair modernity.

Both yours, starting from the Odakyū, at 80 or so kilometres east of Tokyo.

NARITA-SAN SHINJOJI TEMPLE

Off one heads, Odakyū-sen to Yoyogi-Uehara, change to the Chiyoda Line, and on out to Abiko. Another change at Abiko to the Narita Line and then to Narita itself. The few minutes walk from the station takes you past a street of wood-structured shops, more than a hundred of them in all, full of hives and troves of small-sale food, knick-knacks, mementos. Time, however, jumps. This is but

the threshold to Shingon-sect Buddhism begun in 940. The over-whelming centrepiece is the Narita-san Temple, fulcrum and radial gathering-point of the considerable temple complex.

A prayer-to-ancestors stairway. A bell to summon ancestors. Holy incense-smoke. Altars of gold imagery. Lotus motifs. Purple-clad priests. The whole at once stately, a necessary stillness amid the visitors. Two five-storey pagodas give architectural accompaniment, especially the Pagoda of Peace. More is all to hand – the Gaku-dō Hall, the Niō-mon Gate. It may well be crowded during the day, but there is no doubting the invitation to self-space, innerness.

DISNEYLAND

Odakyū to Shinjuku, then Chuo to Tokyo Station. Change to the Keiyo Line and station-by-station southeast to Maihama. Walk, thereafter, or take the Disney Resort Train (*dizuni rizōto train*). Like its fellow sites in California's Anaheim and Florida's Orlando, in Hong Kong and Marne la Vallé in France, this gives you the full works, three huge parks of it. Fantasia in buckets. Mickey and Donald. Snow White. The Shrek generation. You can dive Twenty Thousand Leagues Under the Sea, ride the Big Thunder Railroad, steamboat your way with Mark Twain along the Mississippi, beam yourself up for Star Tours, or visit Cinderella Castle. Floats. Parades. Chirpy music. Children happy, children-in-adults happy.

Since it opened in Urayasu in 1983 it appears to have had 436 mil-lion visitors. On 2009 prices your day-out runs ¥5800 (adult), ¥5000 a junior, and ¥3800 a child. The most successful theme park in the world. Families spend whole vacations at this Disneyland (staying at

Disney hotels). Students speak of their earnest desire to head into Chiba on Disney missions. Multiple visits become a norm. Kim Jong Nam, son of North Korea's Kim Jong Il, was allegedly on his way to Disneyland when deported in 2001. Princess Aiko, the daughter (but not the wished-for son) of Crown Prince Naruhito and Crown Princess Masako, visits in 2006 in order to have a 'normal' childhood. The pundits offer various explanations – a release-valve to Japanese conformity, a recognizable extension to the virtual worlds of Japanese video and manga. Either way Hello Kitty meets Snoopy. No need for innerness here. All is laid on. Hyper-real. Right now.

42

September Tuesday

➲

Odakyū speeds. No mistaking the heavy rhythmic thud of the various Romance Cars. White. Red. Brown, Blue. Especially if you are at either of the two Mukōgaoka-yūen level crossings. Discernible thump. The **Expresses**, at speed, chug more than a touch frenetically. If you are aboard and it is racing, there are several well-known sharp swerves. Brace. Hang on the strap. Grab the hand-rail. Lean on the door. The **Locals**, true to name, have a take-your-time feel. Gentle rail jogs, with longer pauses at some station to let the speeders by (**The Rapid Express, The Tama Express,** the regular **Expresses**). Odd, how after time you get to know by sound what Odakyū train is en route. Train recognition by ear rather than eye. Familiarity. Your train the same?

Given the inevitable occasional Odakyū Line delay (*ressha ga okurete imasu*) due to some technical glitch or the egregious 'personal accident', the company (like all others) has a means of helping 'prove' that lateness for work or class or anything else was the fault of the train service. In Japanese *chien shōmeisho*. A ticket is handed out with marked time-panels saying how much the train has run late. One is supposed to hand in the paper at the workplace or wherever. Nice touch, especially if you really are anxious to make good within office or workplace, Japan after all a society built on punctuality and the clock. Out of interest rather than necessity at Yoyogi-Uehara I took one of the tickets today…it supplies a happy reminder of when you had that cast-iron excuse to avoid school games or *not* to have to attend the dentist.

Music Odakyū? Aboard the **Express** today there was a gathering of school-age youngsters carrying musical instruments. A huge base, violin case (lettered with Tokyo New City Orchestra), and a flute in its own case. Daily you see people following scores with their finger (and occasionally silent-mouthing chorus words). Which makes you think how much music is everywhere attended to and available in Japan. The ubiquitous *karaoke* (literally 'without orchestra') founded in the 1970s by the Kobe musician Daisuke Inoue. *Enka*, that Showa-era massive archive of popular song spanning a 1950s celebrity like Hibari Misora to the recent phenomenon of Jero, an African American in hip-hop dress on TV. J-pop in Harajuku (Namie Amuro's 'Can You Celebrate?' as a two-million musical best-seller or a 'Japanese Idol' male group like SMAP). Classical to be heard on NHK's General Channel 1 concerts, not least under the baton of Seiji Ozawa. Or in the myriads of choirs and recitals, typically at Tokyo's Suntory Concert Hall in Akasaka (Odakyū Line and then the Chiyoda Line). To invoke an old BBC radio broadcast it is Music While You Work.

Odakyū platform feature. Various stations. A red circle and blue circle. Not, as you may think, masonic arcana or boy-scout code. No. Red is where you stand for the first **Express** or **Local** to leave. Blue is for the next **Express** or **Local**, so that you can position yourself to be first into the carriage and thus secure the all-important seat. More space-and-people good train management. More Odakyū good management.

Overhead racks. To be sure they get used by shoppers or travellers heading for other journeys. There is the occasional brief-case, the occasional coat. But the favoured procedure, if seated, is brief-case or bag or backpack on lap, hands forward, head ready for sleep, everything drawn into the sitting-supplicant position. Not a little foetal. Odakyū single cell travel. At once there and not there. Contemplative-Japanese?

43

Odakyū Lady-grooming

➲

First the reach into the handbag for a mirror. Time for make-up. **Maquillage**. Supreme young woman self-absorption. No matter that the rest of us are there. Or that some, as in my own case, are watching like parents at a school play, fashion critics at a catwalk. This is Odakyū-sen as powder-room, beauty salon.

It is the new face-to-be. The face as canvas. A quick tissue wipe. Then, from a galaxy of containers and tubes, the cleanser is called into action. A further and complete facial skin-wipe. After which it is the foundation cream. Rouge, lipstick (plus gloss), eye-liner and eye-shadow (applied with rounded devices that look like adapted spaghetti-pincers), serial dabs of powder. Everything done with the concentrated precision of a Dutch draftsman. A lot of finger smudging of this or that. Endless consultations of the mirror. On a late-night journey the woman in question actually pulled out a battery operated curling machine and got going with that, not something you see too often on a commuter train. Brush, comb and the occasional spatula

as tools-in-trade get wielded, and re-wielded, with practised ease. A drop of eye-lotion or contact lens moistener. A squirt of hair spray.

On you watch, a front-row Odakyū spectator. On the part of the make-up maker-up all has to be accomplished with exquisite timing. After all she would not want to get to her station mid-eyeliner, kind of lop-side black eye to one side, un-lined eye to the other.

Finally this literal self-portrait gets the nod of approval. If there is time to spare there can also be nail-varnish and a touch of filing with just a further minute to get the make-up bottles and tool-kit repacked. And from the train, not infrequently at Shimo-Kitazawa as youth and boutique enclave, out from the train exits your Japanese Hepburn, your elegant railtrack Madonna. If Kafka had been a beautician he might have been proud – an infinite advance on the metamorphosis of your average household cockroach.

Screen-winning performance. Maquillage cinema.

GROOMING VOCABULARY

Mirror	鏡	Kagami
Cleanser	クレンジング	Kurenjingu
Cleansing Lotion	クレンジングローション	Kurenjingu rōshon

Face lotion	化粧水	Keshousui
Foundation	ファンデーション	Fandēshon
Eye-liner	アイライナー	Ai rainā
Eye-shadow	アイシャドー	Ai shadō
Eyebrow pencil	眉ペンシル	Mayu penshiru
Eyelash curler	ビューラー	Byūrā
Eyebrow brush	眉ブラシ	Mayu burashi
Contact lenses	コンタクト	Kontakuto
Tweezers	毛抜き	Kenuki
Mask	マスク	Masuku
Concealer	コンシーラー	Konshīrā
Powder	おしろい	Oshiroi
Rouge	チーク	Chīku
Lipstick	リップ	Rippu
Gloss	グロス	Gurosu
Brush	ブラシ	Burashi
Comb	櫛	Kushi
Hair drier	ドライヤー	Doraiyā
Mousse	ムース	Mūsu
Hair liquid	ワックス	Wakkusu
Curler	カーラー	Kārā
Manicure	マニキュア	Manikyua
Nail file	爪やすり	Tsume yasuri
Nail polish	爪磨き	Tsume migaki

MAQUILLAGE

PRO-ACTIVE – NO.1. GO, GO, GO SOLUTION
KOSÉ – Beauté de Kosé
BIORÉ
VISÉE
COSÉE
KANEBO – NIGHT CREAM AND GELL
KANEBO – FEEL YOUR BEAUTY
BARE ESSENTIALS – BEAUTY CREATION
AUBE
SHISEIDO – BIO-PERFORMANCE, SUPER
RESTORING CREAM
PASTEL SPLASH
ROHTO CLEAR FOR EYE
STREETCOVER
ASIENCE – 'HAIRY TALE' (commercial film for Kao
Cosmetics and Shampoos)
MANDOM – CLEANSING EXPRESS MOIST
LIVIU 21 – GOOD DAYS FOR YOUR LIFE
                         Plus
LUSH – FRESH HANDMADE COSMETICS

44

Odakyū and Near-Odakyū Women's Hairday

➲

HAIRDRESSERS

C'EST LA VIE Cut 3,200 yen
Cold 5,250 yen
Coloring 5,250 yen
Un deux trois

LE PETIT RAPPORT. ÉTIM. HATI – COLLECTION HAIR. ART RUSH. WISH. REMIX. FAVORITE HAIR – Ids. MINX. LA CACHETTE – Hair Suprese. BEAUTRIUM.

RICK. CLIC. MINX. ASH. ZEST. ZAIZA. 1/8 (eight and half). ROMANTIC. FAIRLADY – Hair & Make. KAN-JÉ – Hair Design. PRIS FIXE.
HAIR ZONE – Belle Jouvence. REGALO, BEE-1, AIR SPIRITUS.

45

Odakyū Evenings-out

➲

BUNRAKU

Ourselves just arrived in Japan. A bow into the magnificent puppet art at the National Theatre of Tokyo. Odakyū Line to Chiyoda (Omotesando), and thence, to the Hanzomon Line and station of the same name. The *bunraku* on-stage story is *Yoshitsune and the Thousand Cherry Trees* (*Yoshitsune Sembon Zakura*), first half in the afternoon performance, the second in the evening. Clan plot-line. Warring brothers, with Yoshitsune as hero. Fox magic. Breathtaking puppetry (the manipulators clothed and hooded in black). Puppets in stylized hyper-colour – white visage, pencil-black eyebrows, sumptuous gowning. Subtly tonal *shamisen* accompaniment played with plectrum. All speaking parts ventriloquized through the 'chanter' (*tayū*). Earphone English. To follow, later, will be evenings of *kabuki* at the venerable *kabuki-za* in Ginza which opened in 1889. Plus at the Nerima Bunka Centre (Odakyū Line then change to Oedo Line to Nerima Station) an evening which combines *kyōgen*, a brief, episodic theatre-piece called 'Dondaro', the story of a husband-wanderer's

return, and a stately, meticulous *noh* performance of a classic folk and fox story. But *bunraku* it was as a Japan of First Encounter. An inaugural bow into all the several kinds of 'stage' Japan. *Arigatō.*

DINNER

Evening-after-meeting with colleagues and graduate students. Medium-range Japanese-Japanese restaurant. Tatami-mat room. Long low-tables. Cross-legged dining. *Oshibori* (small hand-cleansing towel) first as in all Japanese eateries. *Hashi* duly horizontal so as not to point to the diner opposite. After an opening *kampai!*, brief speeches, and an *itadakimasu* ('thank you for the meal'), it is on into eats and drinks. Your legs begin to hint of a realm of the dead. Beer (bottle or *nama bīru* – draft beer). *Sake* (rice wine). You pour your neighbour's, your neighbour pours yours. Drinks-at-the-table mutual aid society? Legs fading. Then, in neatest presentation: *otōshi* (Japanese *amuse-bouche*), *chawan-mushi* (savory custard), *yaki-zakana* or *ni-zakana* (grilled or steamed fish), *gohan* (rice – indispensable), *sushi*, *sashimi*, *tempura*, *misoshiru* (miso soup), *hōji-cha* (digestive tea). More speeches still to go and then the *san bon jime*, the final three-times-over ritual hand clap. By now your legs are lost, in the mortuary. Stretch, massage, miracles, a prayer to the *kami* (the shinto spirits). But rising and standing are simply a distant athletic memory. Great evening.

WEDDING

Nothing like Japanese nuptials, not least that the marriage legalities have all actually taken place before the wedding. The betrothed, in truth, have plighted their troth through seal (*hanko*) and signature at their local Ward Office and with due witnesses a week or so earlier. So it is on to the white-gown and formal-suit bash at a quality hotel, in this case the Four Seasons or Chinzan-so. Reachable via Shinjuku, then Yamanote Line to Mejiro, and taxi into the hotel forecourt. Weddings, here, seem to be done every hour on the hour. The ritual is a wonder. Two sets of parents on a dais with the interlocutors, *nakōdo*, in-between. The bride a former student and assistant in the department where one teaches. The bridegroom a dentist, no less. Speeches from friends, even old teachers. Three changes of costume for the new wife at each stage of the banquet. And then, crowning glory, the orgy of photographing. No click more important than those taken of the pair, hand over hand, cutting a huge wedding-cake. But wait. The cake is, well, not a cake, it is a multi-layered plastic replica, with the slice-cut already in place. A wedding, expensively, gloriously, generously, imitating...a wedding. Glad to be a guest.

THE BARD

Shakespeare in Tokyo. A performance of *Macbeth*, dagger and all, at the Globe Theatre. Or rather its round-house replica (full name Panasonic Globe Theatre – built in 1988) at Shin-ōkubo. First, Odakyū to Shinjuku, then one stop along on the Yamanote Line. Vintage Royal Shakespeare Company. Directed by Gregory Doran. Anthony Sher in the title role, a Macbeth shrewdly pitched (and spoken) as resolve and uncertainty. Harriet Walter as sexual, iron-lady Lady Macbeth. So compelling you almost do not want her to make away with herself at the end. Bits of Japanese thrown in to salt the play's English. Small simultaneous-translation devices for Japanese theatre-goers. Could the bard indeed ever have thought that fiefdom Scotland would one day travel to Edo (literally the estuary), the power-centre of another warring clan, that of the Tokugawa (1603-1868)? The same Edo that would in due course be renamed Tokyo (East Capital). One dynastic story for another. One staging for another.

RECITAL

Alicia de Larrocha at Suntory Hall, Akasaka. Piano, pianissimo. But first the Odakyū-sen to Yoyogi-Uehara, then the Chiyoda to Kokkaigijido-mae, with a quick walk to the Suntory Hall. Arrival through the entrance-way – **Herbert von Karajan Platz in ARK Hills.**

Once on stage Mme. Larrocha, a diminutive figure nearing eighty, takes all before her. Quite emphatic virtuosity. Small frame, huge talent. Hers, too, is a name to join other women in the great Catalan musical roster, notably the sopranos Monserrat Caballé and Victoria de los Ángeles. The music soars. Mozart and Hayden, Albéniz and Schumann. A lift to the spirits. But one can not also not react to the setting itself, especially the larger of the two auditoria in its so-called vineyard concert hall design (seats all around the orchestra). Great glass chandelier by Motoko Ishii. Stained glass by Keiko Miura. Wall art by Teppei Ujiyama. The foyer and stage handsome, spacious, in pillars of light-coloured wood. The building's own musical score, as it were.

SPECTACLE

Blue Man Group in Tokyo. The specially constructed Invoice Theatre in Roppongi (Odakyū to Shinjuku, then the Oedo Line to Azabu-juban). *Son et lumière* with a vengeance. Three earless and un-speaking vaudeville-percussionists dressed to appear like blue condoms. Mime. Latex. Choreographed as the uncomprehending movement and stare of child-adults. Aliens. Pumping rock accompaniment. Volcanic paint (the front rows with especially supplied ponchos to catch the splatters). Zithers. PVC tubes. Tuba-like instruments. Drumming straight out of jazz-rock, or Africa, or Venus. Acoustic *thing* language. Maybe musical ciphering. Luminous streamers fire into the audience. Screened cyber-designs and puzzles. Meticulous fades and transformations and always the near autistic-like presence of its performer-three. It is two hours of electronic mural. Visually lavish, and situated in neither Tokyo nor New York nor any known actual geography. Pop Beckett or Pinter land perhaps. The group, the programme brochure and web tell you, grew from 1980s Manhattan art-house, not one but many groups all under the reins of the original trio of Phil Stanton, Chris Wink and Matt Goldman. *Buru-man*, for certain, as is said in Japanese.

JAZZ

Or almost jazz. Piano music pretty much *sui generis*. Namely **Keith Jarrett**. Off we head to The Tokyo Metropolitan Art Space (Odakyū, change at Shinjuku to the Yamanote Line, on to Ikebukuro station). 2000-person concert hall. Jarrett plays standing-up, maybe an aid to concentration as he goes about the improvization of every piece.

A triumph of hitherto un-scored, un-composed musicality. There are, also, the well-known grunts, the pitch and sway of his body, the sense of some personally negotiated contract with the piano. But the pieces, each distinct, discrete, seize the ear. Riffs, harmonies, scales, parallels, inversions. By very definition Jarrett's self-orchestration of piano-key could not be more unique. Most know his cv – the child-prodigy musical ability, the Art Blakey-Miles Davis early years, his multiple recordings and concerts, the different trios and quartets, the Gurdjieff-mystic leanings, and not least his quick-fire intolerance of audience noise or flash photography. But this is a night of regulated performance as befits Japan, with nearly a dozen calls for encores. You see Jarrett in the wings before he returns to the Steinway, music's 'I Gladiator' with towels for brow and face. It is creativity as battleground, music as risk and conquest. The upshot is in-spiriting, a jazz-cum-classical nod towards the spheres.

POETRY

College-venue reading under the title 'Women and Writing'. A bus-ride from Kichijoji (Odakyū to Shimo-kitazawa and on to the Inokashira Line) to *Tokyo Joshi Daigaku*, often abbreviated to *Tonjo* (Tokyo Woman's Christian University). Three poets, myself as MC (that is MC in Japanese usage as taken from English) and a largely student audience. First up is Kazuko Shiraishi who made her bow in the 1960s, the then supposed Bad Girl of Japanese poetry for her 'open' verse of self and city, jazz and sex. Once called 'The Allen Ginsberg of Japan'. Wonderful get-up as always, flying-saucer black hat, multi-colour pants and top. Reads in Japanese and English from her early collection *Tamago No Furu Machi* (*The Town That Rains Eggs*) and *Let Those Who Appear*. Followed by Noriko Mizuta, Chancellor of Josai University in Chiba, translator of Poe, Sylvia Plath and Anne Sexton. Quiet, considerate lyric verse. Then Anne Waldman, four decades a Beat legend. Greenwich Village doyenne and stellar performance poet. Her reading includes a section of *Fast Speaking Woman*, her long-time signature composition. She delivers it as verse-speaking theatre – speed, body, chant. Session over and it is on to dinner and talk.

BISTRO

Minami-Shinjuku, i.e. South Shinjuku (Odakyū Local). Small two-level eatery almost become home from home. From the street a

picturesque flower-decked façade. Run by Japanese husband-and-wife, Toshinori-san (originally from Okinawa) and Miho-san, he a French-speaker from early time spent in Brussels and in the town of Laval of Chateau country. Pays de la Loire. The very choice of name, La Patate, promises the most beckoning culinary bistro-fare – potato, sweet potato, spud. So it proves, whether *dina setto* or *à la carte*. Manageable yen-price. Manageable menu-choice (in Japanese and French). Manageable wine-list (*wainrisuto*). Entrée. Main dish. Dessert. Nothing undue, nothing up-market. Crafted but not over-crafted presentation with Toshinori-san and Miho-san always attentive but never fussing at your shoulder. The place used to have an iron-spiral staircase down to the lower level dining room and toilet/ *toire*. Mid-evening (you might not risk late-evening), and *un verre* too many, and you could begin to regret not having taken out Diners' life (or death) insurance. But that is to take nothing away from this eatery. For there you are, knives and forks rather than chopsticks, and within hailing distance both of Japan's Shinjuku and France's Laval. Eats. Talk. Table-space. *Parfait*. Or in polite Japanese food-parlance *gochisō-sama* ('it was a feast').

46

October Wednesday

Densha de inemuri. Dozing-off. Sleeping. Today, on the **Semi-Express**, I found myself standing next to a salaryman who was snoring, full nostrils. Standing up. No small feat. The ability to get into the Land of Nod on the instant by Japanese passengers is astounding. Sit down. Arrange bag. Hands usually clasped. Head down...and off and away. You can find yourself next to a flat-out, legs splayed, commuter, or the gentle purveyor of zzzzs, or the eyes half-closed dozer. Often a sleeper will land head on your shoulders and you have to exert the polite shove. Either way some magic internal clock operates and at the appropriate station wakefulness takes hold and he or she heads for the carriage-door. A whole lexicon gathers and lingers in your own watching mind. Somnolence. Catalepsy. Narcolepsy. Oneiricism. Trypanosomiasis. Above all the Odakyū as Rip Van Winkle's train dormitory.

Pulling into Seijogakuen-mae we are boarded, among others, by a boy somewhere close to six or eight years of age. Japanese elementary-school pupil. What other culture would allow a near-infant to travel alone in this way? He looks Lilliputian. A tribute to the assumed safety of Japan, and not least its trains. And then there is the kit. All in navy. Military cap with elastic chin-band. Buttoned to the neck tunic jacket. Long short trousers. Black polished shoes and white socks with small blue garter holding them close to knee-caps (the girls have a special leg-glue which keeps their socks up). Above all there is the identifying satchel on the back, in Japanese the *randoseru*, as though the child were some miniature Swiss alpinist. Black leather. Rounded. Shiny. Straps over both shoulders. And with an identity tag plus rail-pass hanging from it. A million small children travel home-to-school-to-home with them. Train-line infancy on the Odakyū.

Heading to Gotokuji on the **Local**. No sooner are we off than a woman faints. Another woman takes hold of her until we reach Shimo-Kitazawa. Then, almost by railway bush telegraph, a platform guard appears and within a trice we have a stretcher. From where?

Subsequently, I discover, it came from a barely noticed cupboard storage space. Obviously it is more than a faint as she is borne off and down the escalator. In the distance, just about, the ambulance siren sounds. All this is done as though pre-rehearsed. Railway medical care on the instant. Formidable.

Odakyū-clothing lingo. Of recently witnessed vintage – Man's black-windjammer simply and starkly bearing the word **HUSTLE**. A woman's red baseball-style coat with the words **BABY, THE STARS SHINE, BABY, THE STARS SHINE**. A boy's padded khaki top reads **EXPRESS DELIVERY**. A thirtyish mother (child in tow) has a skeleton stitched on the back of her jeans in glitter needlework. Youth in low-slung red safari pants has **POWER SOURCE** printed across the seat. Passenger orthography. Passenger badges. Off-the-rack Odakyū.

Almost last **Express** back from Shinjuku to Mukōgaoka-yūen. Full train. Have been meeting visiting academics – a lecture, dinner, likely too much (or too little) sake. Amid returning-home salarymen (also sake-challenged) and assorted youngsters, the mind begins to wander. OER as standing for Only Eat Rāmen? Or a western-literary renaming of the Odakyū. The Milton Romance Car? The George Eliot Tama Express? The Gustave Flaubert Local? Or stations called Seijo-Chaucer, Machida-Goethe, or above all, Shinjuku-Shakespeare? Probably not. Back to personal snooze mode.

47

Odakyū Day-out, Ibaraki

➲

茨城

Off, first, to one of Tokyo's other prime stations, Ueno-eki. Mukōgaoka-yūen to Shinjuku (Odakyū-sen), then Shinjuku (Yamanote-sen) to Ueno-eki. Once there it is all-aboard on the deodorantly-named 'Hitachi Semi Express Fresh' bound for Mito, capital of Ibaraki Prefecture and about 100 kms east and north of Tokyo. But, as you step towards Platform 16 of Ueno station, there is a yet further touch of France-in-Japan. It is the **Wine and Dine** store with its own ripe advertising-French flourish in the window:

Reposons-nous ici. Si on a faim et soif.
Alors on a plusiers choix de bons fromages,
Avec du vin qui fera parfait marriage
Et être avec toi –
Le temps heureux qui me donne la plus grande joie.

Suitably word-fortified you head for your seat, two tickets in hand, one for the journey, one a species of Hitachi receipt. Ninety minutes or so later, having moved from city to countryside, and past mural drawings and a huge communication tower at Ishioka Station and huge oil or grain vats at Tomobe Station, it is arrival at Mito Station. A morning in the city, with trips to the Tokugawa Museum to see something of the shogunate history begun by Shōgun Tokugawa bakufu which ran from 1603 to 1868, and to the beauteous Kairaku-en park and gardens where the annual *ume* or plum festival is held. Our afternoon-and-evening destinations, however, are elsewhere, to two major sites, two contrasting Japans, Kashima Jingu and Tokai Nuclear Power Plant.

KASHIMA JINGU ENTRANCE

Stunning shrine-complex within sight of the port city that shares its name. Shinto. One of the Three Great Shrines of the East (the others are Ikisu in Kamisu, Ibaraki, and Katori in Chiba). Supposedly founded in 660 BC and in honour of the *kami* deity Takemikazuchi-no-mikoto, a god both of martial grace and unity of the people (he helped the Emperor to power).

Set amid over two hundred cherry trees in Kashima Ōgidaira Park.

A whole treasury of sights: the cherry wood gate (*sakura-mon*), the major shrine itself in full Shinto panoply and each subsidiary lesser shrine, the stone lanterns, the deer (*shika*). The annual festival takes place on 1 September. Along with the rest nestles Mitarashi Pond, by repute a body of purificatory water – baptismal font, mirror, bath, a

site to restore and purge the spirit through intimacy with the natural order.

A far, far remove from the Japan of technology and yen.

TOKAI NUCLEAR POWER PLANT (TOKAI GENSHIRYOKU HATSUDENSHO)

Coastal. Japan's first ever nuclear electricity plant. Built in 1961, put into full service 1965, succeeded by a second plant in 1978. Initially a source of national pride, Japan as technological giant.

But then, in September 1999, came a terrible nuclear accident – radiation 20,000 times above normal, families evacuated from within a 350-metre radius, 400 people exposed to radiation, employee deaths. Not a Three Mile Island (1979) or Chernobyl (1986), but dire, serious. If run by a private corporation where was government oversight? How could any citizen not call up, actually or viscerally, the iconic atomic wastelands of Hiroshima and Nagasaki? Do not the very words atom or nuclear carry deep shadows of memory?

Which touchstone had better served, ancient Kashima or modern Tokai?

48

Chikan!
Odakyū Misbehaviour

➲

Herein a sorry business. Groping. Frotteurism. Men behaving badly – though there was recent reported case of a woman alleged to have been shoving and rubbing. But the statistics speak – 4000 men a year arrested nationally, 17% of women travelling by train say they have been molested. The Ministry of Labour receives about 10,000 complaints annually. In 1999, the Keio Line began women-only carriages with the Odakyū Line and others soon there-after following suit. On the Odakyū there are the two carriages usually, one near to the driver's cabin, one near to the guard's. These are so time-tabled for two or two-and-a-half hours each morning and evening. There will always be dangers of false accusation but no-one seriously doubts the problem, not least given packed rush-hour trains. Apart from standard gropes, instances have been reported

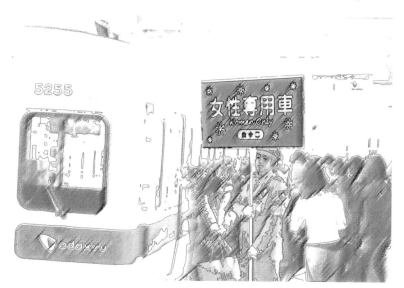

of men biting women's hair. Kind of trichological-dental 'rush' as it were? There are even oddball spin-offs, a Groper's Brotherhood operating as *tomo-no-kai* and a club called *ime-kura*.

Is it deliberate that the notices for these women-only morning and evening carriages are given a pink background? Odakyū in the pink, in lavender, as it were. A 'soft' female image to play against a mean masculine offence?

Allowed into these carriages, however, are 'men with a physical handicap' and 'men who are care attendants'. More phrasing to get you thinking.

One episode that adds its own quirk to the already quirky. TV, and different kinds of consumer event, regularly vaunt the MINISUKA POLICE IDOL GROUP. Essentially this is a dozen-plus attractive young Japanese women dressed in Mother Mary blue rubber or pvc tight mini-outfits – slit skirts (*minisuka* is *romaji* for miniskirt) and caps. Police-themed. Part of their publicity says 'Be arrested by the Minisuka Police'. Not a few men would mind. A combination of Baby Doll, Dominatrix, and Strip-Club Mascot. Frequently referred to as the MINISUKA PORICE. Newspaper for July 2009 report that one of their number, Yukiko Hachisuka, boarded the Odakyū-sen at Shimo-Kitazawa, travelled the line a number of stops, and

found herself subject to groping by a 43-year-old salaryman. The train pulled into none other than Mukōgaoka-yūen, and there, slim-line as may be she valiantly pulled him off the train. The police were called and he was charged and admitted the offence. Known as *genkō taiho* or on-site apprehension. Carriage gender. Carriage justice. Then there is always to hand the police-post, the neighbourhood or corner *kōban*.

On the other hand, as in a 2006 case in which a 17-year-old girl accused a professor on the Odakyū of unwanted fondling and in which the supposed miscreant was caught and apprehended at Shimo-Kitazawa, the issue can also turn murky: the false or unproven accusation. Known as *enzai*. One word against the other. There has even been Masayuki Suo's hit movie, also of 2006, *I Just Didn't Do It*, another story of wrong accusation. But no-one doubts the problem persists. Train malaise. Train misbehaviour.

49

November Thursday

➲

The Odakyū Line, my stretch of it at least, for most of the year has been widening itself. Adding extra track, and with it extra platforms and (over the Tamagawa) a new bridge. Massive, intricate engineering. A near-miracle to watch. City-loads of concrete. Whole snakes of insulated tubing. Earth-movers, fork-lifts, cranes, a cornucopia of vehicles and machinery. Concrete and wooden sleepers. Gravel and pylons. Ready to lay down new rail-tracks. There has been local resident-complaint as old streets get co-opted and demands for underground as against above-ground development, especially near Shimo-Kitazawa. But one feature of the whole operation abides. If you are on an early-morning train, 7.30 a.m. or so, you get a sight of well-ordered files of hard-hat workmen doing… group-stretching. Kind of railway Tai-chi. Or Pilates. Or old-fashioned Calisthenics. Another kind of track (track-suit?) work.

Toire. Toilets. Is there a more luminous name in this realm than TOTO – WC and Urinal? The Odakyū has its full share, station for station. A recent glance at the Toto catalogue brings word and sight of no less than forty-one domestic styles with control-panels worthy of a NASA space shuttle. Heated seats make for the least of it. Super-duper flush valves. High-chrome levers. Skirted bowls. Colours of 'Colonial White' and 'Sedona Beige'. On the Odakyū Line we are talking about urinals which set the logo TOTO either at eye-level or as you look down to roughly crotch-level, together with one traditional 'squat' toilet (*washiki*) alongside the Western variety. Spousal report confirms that in the Ladies toilets also there are rarely paper towels or hot air blowers for after-duty hand-washing as is required form. But then passengers carry small cloth towels or handkerchiefs all the time, for brow-mopping in the summer humidity, for precisely toilet-washroom drying hands duty. Either way TOTO prevails. Odakyū station convenience to meet Nature's call.

Vignette. In the course of four Odakyū (and other Line) trips, a small sartorial gallery. First, a 12 or 13 year-old boy with a baseball cap saying **FUNK YOU** (did his parents know?). Second, a middle-aged lady wearing jeans and a jacket with the splendidly addled inscription **MUSIC MAKES HAPPY HIGHEST HUM.** You cannot beat that. Third, alighting at Mukogaōka-yūen itself, a student-aged youth, with a blue windjammer saying **AQUINAS SOCCER**. Might have challenged the good Dominican Church father himself, Dr Angelicus. After all there's not much mention of ball-dribbling, goal-mouths, or corner-kicks in the *Summa Theologica* (1265–1274). His tome's dates, even so, half-resemble a bit of Odakyū train time-tabling.

Can any country have more considerate arrangements for the dis-abled on their metro-trains? The station calls ahead to say that a dis-abled passenger is looking to board or leave the train. A small iron platform-to-train bridge is pulled out, on or off rolls the wheelchair. Due care and attention. Kind words are exchanged. The blind, like-wise, have available indented yellow guide-tracks in every station (*Ki iro i sen*). Platform braille. Odakyū does yet more duty by key groups of passengers

November cold. The **Local** had a timetabled pause at Izumi-Tamagawa to allow for other trains to pass. The conductor makes the announcement that a good half of the train doors will be closed to keep in the heat. Something parallel happens in the Summer – a number of doors, not all, are closed to keep in the air-conditioning. Yet more best train etiquette.

50

Odakyū Blues

➲

THIRTEEN WAYS OF LOOKING

Any Odakyū station or train-train-window opens a mosaic of blue to you. It is a colour that weaves into the very texture of Japanese life – sky or river reflection to be sure, but also things, objects, materials. Nothing if not one of the Line's primary colours. Wallace Stevens's poem, 'Thirteen Ways of Looking at a Blackbird', supplies the perfect conjugation.

1. Almost all buildings under construction or being repaired are covered in blue tarpaulin, It is as though it were skin. Currently under blue are a bank near Kyodo, a post office near Seijo, road work near Shin-Yurigaōka, and various housing complexes alongside the track (of the kind first built in the 1950s and known as *danchi*).

2. Crossing the Tamagawa Bridge in summer, weekends especially, the eye alights on the picnickers – seated on or standing by their blue tarpaulin spreads. Almost invariably there is a *hibachi*, a round or square iron grill, with chicken or meat sizzling.

3.   Odakyū Line carriages, **Local or Express**, have their own hori-
     zontal blue strip mid-position against the rest in cream or sil-
     ver. They could easily serve as a kind of railway bar-code, the
     type seen on books or store items. Each, too, has the painted-on
     white Odakyū logo.

4.   No station would be fully dressed if it did not have a drinks
     machine, SUNTORY (which has Tommy Lee Jones sponsoring
     BOSS coffee), ITO EN, POKKA, DYDO, YAKULT, KIRIN
     and ASAHI among others. The last, in the shape of an upturned
     cereal-packet, is a metal shell with library shelves of vitamin
     drinks, sodas, water, tea and coffee. And painted in blue. Drinks
     blue.

5.   Approach a ticket gate on the Odakyū and you have four fea-
     tures in blue: a blue square as decoration, a blue surround on
     the IC small screen where the ticket is placed, a pair of blue
     rubberized turnstile-panels that snap open when you use your
     ticket and a white-on-blue circle with the instruction in Japa-
     nese and English 'Please walk slowly'. Add to these the blue
     ticket-machines themselves.

6.   Odakyū-store plastic bags. Several sizes and strengths. Blue
     writing with due Odakyū logo on white background. Portable
     blue-on-white. Shopping blue-on-white.

7. As your Odakyū travel eye settles on which train–at–a–glance familiarity, colour again plays its role. Even at a distance you spot Red for **Express**, Magenta for **Tama Express**, Green for **Semi-Express** and two blues: Light Blue for **Semi-Section Express** and Regulation Blue for **Local**.

8. Carriage wall diagrams in blue. No speaking on the phone. Yield your seat to the elderly or pregnant. Sit out of disturbance range of your neighbour. Each of these is accompanied by Odakyū written instructions – also in blue. All in blue.

9. Station name signs. Quite apart from the pluri-language there is yet another Odakyū blue strip through each. Visual decoration maybe, a touch of linear design maybe. But does not each also exactly parallel the rail track itself?

10. March 2008 saw the latest Romance Car introduced. The 60,000 (MSE). Streamline Blue. Barrels up and down the Odakyū track Hakone-Yoyogi-Uehara-Kita-senju (the Chiyoda route to Chiba). Like its **Limited Express** five train-confrères, it offers colour-in-motion. Blue-in-motion. It was also given the Blue Ribbon Award by the 3500-member Japan Railfan Club, meeting in Shinjuku, in 2009 as 'best new car'.

11. The Odakyū is accompanied by whole clothes-lines of wire. Overhead electricity for the train, endless cabling alongside. Saul Sternberg geometry from any of his *New Yorker* covers.

As the track has been widened it now has whole stretches in
blue. Lines out for a walk. Blue lines.

12. Odakyū Store blue. Each of the stores, Shinjuku and Machida
notably, has its name emblazoned in capital-letter English, under-
lined, and in Japanese underneath. But what adds a point of style
is that the A in ODÂKYŪ has a pink circumflex-like mark over
it. Designer-blue with pink trimming. Nice touch.

13. Mukōgaoka-yūen station, north and south entrances, carries its
own blue name-inscription. Oblong. Left side has blue Odakyū
logo on white backdrop, then the rest of the backdrop eases into
blue with the station-name in 'bold' Japanese and *romaji*. Ticket
machines, the blind strip, lockers, electronic time-table, turn-
stiles. Classic small-station Odakyū. Blue Odakyū.

51

Odakyū Men's Haircut

➲

**strange synthetic perfumes
Unguent, powdered, or liquid**
T.S. Eliot, '*The Waste Land*'

Hair-care. This past decade tonsorial attention to my thinning pate has been in the hands and scissors of yet another husband-and-wife pair. And no more than a stone's throw from Mukōgaoka-yūen station. They run the ground-floor barbers of a small corner house, the door emblazoned with the English word 'Enter'. You know when they are in business (no Mondays) as they have one of those old-fashioned revolving red, white and blue barber's poles. They speak no English and my own Japanese can in no way stretch even close to 'please trim the eyebrows' or 'I'd rather not have any spray thank you' – though I can say *mijikai* ('short'). Hair style with a side parting, too, I have learned is known in Japanese as a 7:3. From the opening *konnichiwa* to the closing *arigatō*, and by gestures, smiles and pointing, we have managed to ease ourselves into a fond trans-linguistic client and professional routine. It is a full hour, whatever

your own paucity of thatch, a ceremonial interlude of aprons and shampoo, razors and massage. Worthy of a small verse epic, a BBC or PBS documentary. Never mind *Hair*, the 1960s hippie-musical. What about *Hair*, the Japanese operetta, the Japanese *tanka*? It bears observation that, round the corner, a rival establishment is called simply **BAR BER**, the coincidental middle-spacing you have to feel just as it should be. Drinks and a trim?

In you go, mutual bows, coat on hanger, a barber-seat if free – otherwise a small corner seat with either TV to watch or radio talk-show to remind you that this truly is *Nihon* and not London or New York. On one occasion, and almost on cue, a local came in wearing a baseball cap inscribed with the words 'Wall paper for the corner'. Your turn, next, and once seated in the operating-chair, it is all systems go, hands-on. Cut and trim, wash and dry, shave and after-shave. Yours, the whole shebang, for ¥4000. So into a nearby small pot go spectacles and off we launch.

First you get the in-for-an-operation apron treatment. Not one but two covering aprons, and just to be sure, a third one of plastic not unlike the rubber coverings you get when having an X-ray. Suitably insulated it is on to the slightly perfumed water-spray, preparation for the first scissors-trim. This comes out of one of the several rubber tubes connected to an Espresso Coffee-like machine on the other side of the room. The husband-barber, if he is doing the scissoring, then gets into a kind of dance-routine. He cuts, surveys his work, raises the other hand in the air, each time slightly stomping himself into position. A touch of the tango. The wife-barber, care itself, does slightly less of the light fantastic though she is a positive vampire when it comes to shovelling up spent hair from the floor. Both resort to an endless supply of scissors, garden shears to cuticle size.

Hai dōzo. The first of many 'please' invitations. This one, after the general cut, is the lean into the wash-bowl, helped by whichever barber, and where you get a next spray-surge of hot water. Then it is time for the shampoo, delivered from an industrial white plastic container. Serious application. Rubbed in with a vengeance. Fingers poking hard against the skull. A nail brush goes over your skull and I imagine my own all too compliant follicles being ripped from their sockets like cowardly weeds. The bottles invite some wonderment. The big ones are labelled COLOR STORY with subtitles of COND and MOU. They come not only in white, but blue, pink, and an alarming lime-green. You also begin to take on the look of some ancient Persian potentate in a turban of white foam. Once hair-cleansed it is more water-spray then a towelled head rub as vigorous as 6 a.m. army calisthenics. Another *hai dōzo*, another guiding touch of the elbow, and you are back upright in the chair gazing at yourself in the mirror under a (usually yellow) crown-to-brow towelette. More turban.

Next the arm vibrator. Something that resembles a miniature earth-mover is applied to your arms and shoulders. Shake and bake. Quite what benefit it confers is beyond me but there is no denying a certain gymnastic tingle, the sense that some nerve or ligature is having good done to it. It also is run over your head. But that is not all. Next comes the heavy roller, a *Terminator* gadget, which does your back. Side to side. A near upper-body tremor (I was once in the chair when a minor Tokyo quake occurred – the small rattle of bottles, the momentary tilt of scissors). Once again you have to feel that some kind of bodily health-return is being elicited. Quite what is uncertain. Why ask? Finally there is neck-muscle manipulation and a bit of literal back-slapping rather in the manner of a Buddhist master hitting the novice. Again you have to assume this is good for the metabolism. Or something.

Now comes bed-time. Not so in truth but the chair is tilted horizontal with yourself face-up and eyeing the ceiling. At this point most Japanese clients close their eyes and nod off. Many is the time I have heard rhythmic nasal ins-and-outs, barbershop snores. I certainly close the eyes and go into a hair half-realm. Wheeled to your left side is a small-crane or arm out of which issues more perfumed steam, a seeming Turkish-bath tube. While this is happening a white and chilled face mask appears. Pure Hannibal Lector. Eyes, nose and mouth holes. Carefully it is put into place – to help the skin I assume as it is soaked in a latest unguent. And there you lie, more Egyptian than Iranian prince this time and ready to travel into the next world. In reality it is still your own decked-out self though in décor you would not want photographed for a family album.

A while on, and your *Phantom of the Opera* mask removed, it is shave-time. Cream (again with a hint of sweet hospital-aroma about it) is applied, followed by yet another hot towel, then a pause, and then surgery begins. Open razor. Head to the right, head to the left. Japan was my first-ever site of being shaved by a barber and initially the prospect of a lethal blade near to eyeball and nose had me cringeing. But I have become a veteran, more than pleased to feel every nook and cranny whisker getting its crop. That done, and a touch of precision razor-work on the sideburns, it is more hot towels and on to the satellite hair – eyebrows, nose, and ear. Each has its own implement, especially the ears where a whirring device hovers just at the entrance. That, too, initially, had me edging into fear. Dim memories kept dredging up of ear-biology – canal, tympanic membrane, ossicles, cochlea. Not to worry. Both barbers are virtuosi, dexterity personified at nasal and ear hair removal and at outer-wax hunting. More scented towel-action and then it is back into upright position for the final manicure.

Scrupulous combing. A pump-action squirt of some species of mousse. Final hair-sculpture snips here, there, by scissors and razor. Lots of hair dryer action. A final round of hair spray. A final bit of towel action. Glasses re-nosed and mirror to mirror inspection. Bows. Arigatōs. Brush-down. And, half dizzy from so much lying down, out comes wallet for payment. The money is placed on a small tray, then put by husband or wife into the cash register, and gift society to the last, you are offered either a single cigarette or a single wrapped piece of candy. With the candy in pocket, on with coat and a final *arigatō*. Bow and into the street. Even if the nearby shop windows reflect your Western face you can not help wanting to say *nihonjin-desu* ('I am Japanese').

This has been a hair close-encounter to set a standard. Samson without loss of power. Japanese Vidal Sassoon. A head of hair as marshalled as it has ever been. I could bow in all directions. The Confucian acolyte. The Shinto believer. The Buddhist supplicant. In actuality no more than a cleaned-and-polished *gaijin* boasting a decent haircut.

52

Odakyū Day-out, Ō-Sumo

◗

Actually not so much a day-out as a day-in. Fifteen of them, in fact, and likely best to be described as virtual days-out. Sumo by TV, courtesy of NHK (*Nippon Hōsō Kyōkai*) – Japan Broadcasting Corporation.

For this is Japan's emblematic sport. The *rikishi* or wrestlers themselves. Huge, stately male bodies, rippled in surface fat but sheer muscle tonnage beneath. Clad in *mawashi* or belt, black, blue, red, silver and the like. Oiled hair in the form of a top-knot or *chonmage*. The *shinpan* or judges invariably former *rikishi*. The *gyoji* or umpire in Shinto-style costume and each with his *gunbai* (originally a war-fan) in hand. The *yobidashi*, a kind of sumo civil-servant who sweeps the sand smooth, calls out the wrestlers' names, and wields the *hyoshigi* or clappers.

A sport steeped in ritual, from the *shinto* shrine awning with its hanging *gohei* or white paper zig-zags to the *dohyō* (the circular fight-ring marked by rice-bale rope). Everything counts – the

makunouchi dohyō-iri or ring-entering ceremony with the wrestlers in their apron insignia, the endorsements carried round the ring in flag-parade manner, the purifying salt thrown into the *dohyō* by each wrestler, the chanted names. The bows. The acts of respect. *Shiko* or foot stamping at the beginning of a bout, left leg then right leg raised and lowered. All this and more between the *yokozuna* as Grand Champion performing the *unryu-gata dohyō* or opening ceremony in his *tsuna* or white hemp belt through to the *kimigayo*, the closing national anthem, and the presentation of the massive Emperor's Cup. An NHK interview with the winner of each *basho* or tournament invariably follows. That is naturally in Japanese, but for myself, and other *gaijin*, also given in yet more English translation. Imagine an English-language network doing a parallel service – Japanese commentary in a US broadcast on US football or in an Australian broadcast on cricket with translation of arising interviews.

TV sumo in Japanese is all yours throughout the whole of fifteen afternoons. But come 4 p.m. until 6 p.m., and if you switch to the satellite sub-channel of BS2, it is English-language commentary for the rest of the broadcast. This is to share the same screen with your Japanese fellow sumo-philes but to do so in un-same idiom. A whole consortium of Englishes to be heard: American, Hawaiian, Australian, British, European (in the once-in-a-while voice of the Czech or other ambassador) and even Japanese (in the person of a

well-known singer who speaks English). The phenomenon becomes
a fascination almost of a kind with the sport in view.

Once you get watching, and hooked, it does not take long to start
learning sumo-speak as if to the manner born. Japanese. Japanese-
into-English. You pick up that there are the six *basho* a year (three in
Tokyo, the others in Osaka, Nagoya and Fukuoka). You learn about
the classic eras and fighting names (*shikona*) as against birth names
– Taiho, Chiyonofuji and Wajima in the 1970s–1980s, Takanohana,
Akebono and Musashimaru from the 1990s (the latter two Hawaiian), and the sumo's Bad Cop/Good Cop Mongolian pair of *yokozuna* – Asashoryu (now forced to resign) and Hakuho. You learn
about the *banzuke* as the ranking list, the *ōzeki* as one-down from the
yokozuna, and the hierarchy of divisions, *sanyaku*, *jūryō* and *makushita*. You learn about the *tachiai* as the opening charge, the *yotsu* grip
when the two wrestlers fall into a mutual clasp, the *mono ii* when
there is a dispute about who has won. You start to understand the
techniques. *Yorikiri* and *Oshidashi* as the two commonest kinds of
push-out. *Tsukitaoshi* when the opponent is knocked to the ground.
Shitenage for an over-arm throw. *Okuri-taoshi* for a rear push. On, it
unfolds, even the sound of the *mawashi* or belt being slapped. A huge,
intricate procession of custom, history, language.

If you live in Tokyo it would not be hard to make your way to
the arena, the *Ryōgoku kokugikan* (Odakyū, then JR Sobu Line to
Ryōgoku Station). Once in a while you do.

But the allure of a comfortable seat, right beverage, and the camera
eye patrolling the proceedings, is hard to resist. Plus you understand
the commentary. So it is indeed time and occasion for **SUMO
ENGLISH**, the plait of different Native Speaker voices. The cast-
line, all unseen as NHK chooses only to have you hear but not see
the commentators, becomes a voice-family, intimate play-by-play
auditory companionship. Key names who you come to recognize on
the instant include:

DAVE WIGGINS

Rush Limbaugh voice. Longtime US and Hawai'i sports writer-
broadcaster. Just retired. All over the microphone, shouty, volu-
ble, a main man for the sumo-fanatic. His phrases have passed into
sumo-English legend – 'Holy Toledo' or 'That was smash-mouth
sumo.' None, however, more summons the crash-to-clay demise
of a given *rikishi* than 'Get out the maple syrup, Grandma, it's
pancake time.'

DOREEN SIMMONS

British queen-consort, or maybe queen-mother, of sumo commentary since 1992. There's not a thread of a *gyoji*'s costume she has not studied or a third step-cousin of Takanohana she hasn't met. You can still hear the Nottingham in her voice, despite her Cambridge degree in English. Apart from her sumo duties she is a translator in the Diet and has played Miss Marple on various audio-versions of Agatha Christie.

ROSS MIHARA

Hawai'i-raised commentator, full of eye-on-the-bout good observation and a winning chuckle. Kind of point-man for the commentary. His voice takes on an especial warmth when he brings in other Team Hawai'i commentary, whether that of his helpfully bi-lingual fellow broadcaster **Hiro Morita**, or the gutturally-challenged Takamiyama (Jesse James Wailani Kuhaulua – the first foreign *rikishi* to rise to the top division), or the wry, engagingly offbeat Musashimaru (Fiamalu Penitani – actually Samoan-Hawaiian).

MURRAY JOHNSON

Australian fluency itself. Barely loses a stride. Quick to seize on the bout's moves and momentum. Rarely takes off in other directions about sumo tattle or gossip. Perfect man for the job in the sense that he knows sumo technique, always has a fistful of statistics about past records, and neither over-intrudes nor leaves undue gaps or silences.

Add to these a further gallery. Two Britishers: the laconic, mono-tonal Britisher **Clyde Newton** who edits *Sumo World*, and **Stuart Atkin**, the genially disposed expert on *The Tale of Genji*. Also long seasoned American sumo-hands like **David Shapiro**, author of *Sumo: A Pocket Guide* (1995), and **Mark Schilling**, author of *Sumo: A Fan's Guide* (1994), along with **Ken Swensen**. Or the various female commentators – the Australian **Katrina Watt**, now returned to her own country, who rarely hid her affection for the sport, or **Lynn Matsuoka**, whose sumo line-drawings and full-scale paintings have become frequent book illustrations and are to be seen in her Tokyo gallery. Or the English-speaking Reiko Matsumoto who does all the *hanamichi* reports (the *hanamichi* is the corridor leading from the sumo changing rooms to the ring) and translations of the *rikishi* interviews.

To hand, or rather to ear, is sumo always in its own Japanese right but also as a wondrous English-language consortium. Sumo as more than simply a broadcast, but a language-school, a colloquium, a UN translation booth.

Sumo on TV
Sumo on bikes
Sumo on the street
Sumo on the air
Sumo days-out
Sumo days-in
Sumo
ō-sumo

53

December Friday

➲

Odakyū train skills, especially on the **Local** or **Semi-Express**, or **Section Semi-Express**, require that you get to know which side to stand on if you want to avoid being buffeted at every stop. You need to be on the side that is opposite to the one where the door opens. If, then, you can wedge yourself into the niche between the handrail and that door, you can prevent getting pushed about. A bit like everyone aiming to get the end seat so you have only one passenger next to you. The rules of carriage 'military' engagement, as it were. You have to be on the top of your game, train-stop savvy. Odakyū travel tactics. Odakyū seatsmanship.

Gōtokuji through to Seijo, on the way home. It is time for the male equivalent of the New York bag lady. A slightly shabby type, raincoat grease-spotted, he hurtles through the carriage, scouring each overhead rack. He is on a **MANGA-HUNT**. A train ferret. Two heavy carrier bags bear his paper loot for the day. Quite imperturbable. Single in focus. Eyes keen. He discards the odd newspaper, the odd bits of publicity, but reaches up for anything akin to a book-story. Odakyū's own literary spot-trader? An updated version of the Victorian novelist's 'Dear Reader'? Who knows? 40%, of all published material in Japan, I learn, is *manga*.

Mukōgaoka-yūen south-to-north level crossing. Two trains momentarily poised at the stations, one Shinjuku-bound, the other Enoshima-bound. The barriers are raised high as we head across. Just in front of me I see a fairly sizeable Japanese man pushing his bike. He is wearing jeans, sneakers, and a burgundy-coloured jacket with the word **ARMAGEDDON** in large black capital letters. You look at the two trains, ready-to-go tensile metal, likely to make the level crossing bump some as they heave out of the station, and you have to think 'warning'. The gods indeed. Touchstone Pictures indeed. Possible Armageddon indeed. Nothing if not train and rail-track Wagner.

Few Japanese novels, or novels-into-films, have captured a cultural sense of the railway as intimacy than *Poppoya* – originally a 1997 story-cycle in eight parts by Asada Jirō and then a 1999 film with the lead taken by the well known actor Ken Takakura. The Odakyū line is a far cry from Jirou's Hokkaido country station setting, but like other Japan lines it exerts its own power of association. There is a heavy dose of sentimentality in *Poppoya* (the title means railway-man), but it awakens wholly symptomatic seams of affection, and recognition, in most Japanese hearts. The synopsis for the film version runs as follows: Otomatsu Sato has devoted his entire life to the railroad, first as a boiler-man, then as station-master in the tiny boom town he calls home. But the rail line is due to be scrapped, and the youth are leaving for the cities. As he muses on the dying town, Sato's mind turns on the sacrifices he has made in putting his duty before his family, and to what remains of his future.

TV news brings word that the Zero Series Shinkansen, begun in 1964 (and calling at Shin-Osaka and Hakata among other stops) is being withdrawn completely. The so-called 'Dream Express'. Bullet nose. White-blue colour. Interviewees speak as though it were an elderly relative being put into a nursing home. Who can be more custodial about their trains than the Japanese? The Odakyū, the sardine-can, as reported, now has its new Type 60,000 MSE. No wonder my own affection for the line has become unyielding. A perfect note on which to round out this month-for-month Book of Train Days (not to say Nights).

54

Odakyū Store

➲

小田急ストア

Shopping Guide to Shinjuku Odakyu Department Store
小田急百貨店 新宿店のご案内

SELECTIVE FLOORS

Photographing is not allowed in this store without permission.
PLEASE CONTACT OUR STAFF IF YOU WANT.

Odakyu Carillon Golf School (Reception Desk Located on the 7th
floor of Halc building)
小田急カリヨンゴルフスクール（受付：ハルク7 階）
ビックカメ
Halc Sports (Sporting Apparel and Equipment/ Horse Riding
Equipment)
Bic Camera
ハルクスポーツ（スポーツウェア・用品/乗馬用品）
ビックカメラ

Music, School Uniforms
音楽 学生服
Gourmet Alley
グルメアレー
Manhattan Hills Restaurant District
レストラン街 マンハッタンビルズ
Books, Stationery, Arts, Eyewear
美術 額装 書籍 文具 メガネ 補聴器
Baby/ Kids Apparel, Toy, Child's glasses
ベビー・こども服 玩具 こども用メガネ
Formal, Lingerie/ Nightclothes, Women's Apparel (Big and Petite Sizes)
婦人服 婦人ブラックフォーマルウエア 大きなサイズ・小さなサイズの婦人服
婦人肌着・ナイトウエア ビューティーケア ウイッグ
International Boutiques
インターナショナルブティック

RESTAURANTS

Nada Man-hinkan (Japanese) 14F
「日本料理 なだ万賓館」
Ginza Seigetsudo (Casual French cuisine) 14F
「気軽なフランス料理 銀座 清月堂」
Ristorante Machiavelli (Italian) 13F
「リストランテ マキャベリ」
Kaikaboh (Korean seasonal variety dishes) 12F
「韓国旬彩料理 妻家房」
Toh-anka (Chinese dining) 12F
「チャイニーズダイニング 桃杏花」
Futaba (Eels) 12F
「うなぎ 双葉」
Mugiboshi by Grill Mantensei (Western style grill) 12F
「洋食 麦星 by グリル満天星」
Bon Lien (French Cuisine) 8F
「フレンチレストラン ボン・リアン」
Canterbury Café (House of fine coffee, healthy juices, and cakes) MB3F
「おいしい珈琲と健康ジュースとケーキの店 カンタベリカフェ」
Shinjuku München (Beer pub) B3F
「ビアレストラン 新宿 ミュンヘン」

Please feel free to ask clerks nearby or information desk for support to locate your lost company in our facilities.

Feeding room, baby seat for changing diapers, hot water apparatus etc. are all available. Baby changing stations are also available for your convenience.
Senior carts are available for our customers requiring special care. (It is available for the use within our facility during our store hours only.)

Shinjuku Station Underpass
新宿駅コンコース

Odakyū Bookshelf

➲

Ramón Vilaró, *Japón: Más Allá del Vídeo y las Geishas* (1988)
Alan Booth, *The Road to Seta: A 2000-Mile Walk Through Japan* (1990)
Clive Collins, *Sachiko's Wedding* (1991)
Karl Taro Greenfield, *Speed Tribes: Days and Nights with Japan's Next Generation* (1994)
Richard Hosking, *A Dictionary of Japanese Food: Ingredients & Culture* (1996)
Suzanne Kamata (ed), *The Broken Bridge: Fiction from Expatriates in Literary Japan* (1997)
Benôit Peeters et Fréderic Boilet, *Tokyō Est Mon Jardin* (1997)
Robin Gerster, *Legless in Ginza* (1999)
Peter Tasker, *Samurai Boogie* (1999)
Alex Kerr, *Dogs and Demons: Tales of the Dark Side of Japan* (2002)
Michele Camandona, *A Est di Tokyo* (2003)
Gerald Vizenor, *Hiroshima Bugi: Atomu 57* (2003)
Ivan Vartanian and Lesley A. Martin, *Graphiscape Tokyo* (2003)
Donald Richie, *A View From the Chuo Line* (2004)
Michael Ferrier, *Kizu: La Lézarde* (2004)
Tokyo: Petits Portraits de l'Aube (2004)
Mo Hayder, *Tokyo* (2004)
Peter Carey, *Wrong About Japan: A Father's Journey With his Son* (2005)
Peter and Renate Giacomuzzi (eds), *Nach Japan: Reiselesebuch* (2005).
David Peace, *Tokyo Year Zero* (2007)
Amélie Nothomb, *Ni d'Éve ni d'Adam* (2007)
Mark Gresham and A. Robert Lee, *Japan Textures: Sight and Word* (2007)

Last Train

Glossary

➲

aisu kōhī, iced coffee
Akachan-Anshin-Onakama-Hoikushitsu, Safe Place for Babies and
    Friends (local kindergarten)
Amuro, Namie, pop star of the hit song 'Can You Celebrate?'
apāto, apartment
arigatō gozaimasu, thank you very much
arubaito, part-time work
Asahi Shimbun, Japanese daily newspaper
Ashinoko, Lake Ashi

barabara jiken, scattered parts incident. Body that has been cut into
    pieces.
Bashō, Matsuo (1644-94), haiku master and author of *Oku no Hoso-
    michi*, *The Narrow Road to the Interior*
bento, prepared lunch-box
biru, beer
bōnenkai, end of year party. Literally 'forget the year' party.
bonsai, art of growing miniature tree-shaped decorative plants
bōshi, hat
bunraku, traditional puppet theatre
bushidō, samurai warrior code of swordsmanship and honour
Buson, Yosa (1716–1784), haiku poet and painter

cha (or *o-cha*), tea
chawan-mushi, savory custard
Chiba-ken, Chiba Prefecture
Chigusa,Yokohama jazz club
chikan, groping, groper
Cui-dore Taro (Kuidaore), much loved Osaka restaurant mascot

Daily Sports, newspaper
Daily Yomiuri, The, daily English language newspaper
deijii, daisy
deguchi, exit
depāto, department store
dizuni rizōto train, Disney Resort train

do itashi-mashite, you're welcome
dohyō, sumo arena
dōmō arigatō, thank you very much
dori, main road or thoroughfare

ebi, shrimp, prawn
eigo ichi, first year English
eki, station
eki bento, station lunch-box usually eaten on train
eki kakariin, train station and platform personnel
enzai, unwarranted accusation

Fuji-san, Mount Fuji
furisode, decorative long-sleeved kimono

gaijin, foreigner
Gan, usually translated as *The Wild Geese*, classic Ogai Mori novel
genkō taiho, on-site arrest or apprehension
ginkō, bank
gochisō-sama, great, wonderful. Literally 'it was a feast'.
goihei, white zig-zag purificatory symbols (usually paper)
gomen-nasai, sorry
gomi, rubbish, trash, garbage
gyōza, pork and cabbage dumpling

habotan, small, green-purple cabbage-like flowers
hai dōzo, yes, please
haiku, classic 17-syllable poem
Hakone-Yumoto, Odakyū Line terminal
hanko, portable name seal
hashi, chopsticks
Hikawa Maru, ocean liner now permanently anchored by Yamashita
    Park, Yokohama
Hilton Tokyo, The, leading Japanese hotel near Shinjuku Station
hiragana, writing system using syllabic characters for native words
Hiroshige, Utagawa (1797–1858)
Hōchi Shimbun, Japanese daily sports newspaper
hōji-cha, digestive tea
Hōryuji Temple, wooden Buddhist temple in Ikaruga, Nara, dating
    back to 747AD
Hōsō Daigaku, Open University
Hyatt Regency, leading Japanese hotel near Shinjuku

IC, Intelligent Card. For railways, buses, small purchases, etc.
Igirisu-jin, English person
irasshaimase, welcome
iriguchi, entrance
irowake, separate colours
Isetan, well-known department store
itadakimasu, Bon appétit. Literally 'shall gratefully take it'
izakaya, pub, bar, literally "liquor store where you linger"

Japan Herald, first ever English language newspaper in Japan
Japan Times, The, daily English language newspaper
jidō kaisatu, train ticket gate
jidō kenbaiki, train ticket machine
jinshin jiko, 'personal accident' usually meaning train suicide
Jonasan, Jonathans
JR, Japan Railways
jyusu, juice

kabuki, traditional and vividly staged drama
Kabuki-za, Ginza historic kabuki theatre
Kabukicho, Shinjuku East Exit strip bar, massage parlour and red-
    light district
kaiseki, exquisitely prepared and presented meal
kami, Shinto spirits
kanji, writing system using Chinese characters
kanko ōtō, train and platform system of call and response
Karakida, Odakyū Line station terminal
karaoke, sing-along music and video entertainment. Literally 'without
    orchestra'.
karasu, crow
Kashima Jingu, Kashima Shrine, Ibaraki
katakana, writing system using syllabic words (for loan words)
Kawasaki-shi, city in Kanagawa province
Keio Plaza, leading Japanese hotel near Shinjuku Station
keitai/keitai denwa, portable or cell phone
Kentakkī furaido chikin, Kentucky Fried Chicken
kiiroi sen, yellow indented strips to guide the blind or visually impaired
kimigayo, Japanese national anthem
kōban, police box or small station
kōhī, coffee
Koizumi, Junichirō, Japanese Prime Minister (2001–2006)
kome, rice

konbini, convenience store
konnyaku, edible water plant
kōshinjin, monkey shrine
Kuan Di Miao, historic Yokohama Chinatown temple
kudasai, please
Kumonosu-jo English title, *Throne of Blood*, classic Akira Kurosawa film
kyōgen, short comic form of Japanese theatre that often accompanies Noh.

Lumine, Japanese department chain-store

Maihime, usually translated as *The Dancing Girl*, Ogai Mori classic novel
Mainichi Shimbun, Japanese daily newspaper
Makudonarudo, McDonalds
manga, serial cartoon-stories in book form. Literally 'whimsical pictures'
manshon, literally mansion but meaning a block of apartments, condomium, or flats
matsuri, shrine festival and worship
Meiji-era (1868-1912), named for the Emperor Meiji
mijikai, short (for haircut)
mineraru wō-tā, mineral water
minka, traditional Japanese building style
misoshiru, miso soup
mizu, water, often given the honorific 'o' as in o-mizu
Mizuho, leading Japanese bank
Mocambo, Yokohama jazz club
Mori, Ogai (1862-1922), Japanese novelist, poet and physician
moshi, moshi, phone-answering hello
Mukōgaoka-yūen, author's local Odakyū line station
Musashino-kan, Shinjuku cinema
Mylord, Japanese department chain-store
Myth of Tomorrow, huge Taro Okamoto mural in Shibuya Station

nakōdo, interlocutor, go-between (for a wedding), speechmaker at the wedding
nama bīru, draft beer
Nambu Line, line connecting to the Odakyū at Noborito station
Narita Airport, principal Tokyo airport, 1 hour 20 mins from Tokyo by Narita Express Train.

Narita-shi, Narita city
New Treasure Island, landmark pirate-story manga by Osamu Tezuka published in 1946
NHK, Nippon Hōsō Kyōkai, Japanese Broadcasting Corporation
ni-zakana, fish gently simmered in broth
Nihon, Japan
Nikkei Sports, Japanese daily sports newspaper
niku manjū, buns made of pork filling, usually abbreviated to niku-man
nira, vegetable, flat-leafed member of the onion-garlic family
No.1, leading Japanese travel agency

Odakyū Azur, Odakyū cosmetics outlet
Odakyū-Ox, Odakyū Line kiosk
Odakyū-sen, Odakyū Line
Odawara, Odakyū Line station terminal
Oku no Hosomichi, The Narrow Road to the Interior, major work by Bashō, based on his journey by foot to Honshu in 1689. Written version completed in 1694. Published posthumously in 1694.
omamori, shrine good luck charm
onigiri, rice ball or sandwich in edible seaweed wrapping
oshibori, small hands-cleansing towel for before meals
ō-sumo, polite form of saying sumo, Grand Tournament sumo
otōshi, amuse-bouche

pachinko, pinball-style game using slots and balls in parlours everywhere in Japan
pasmo, all-purpose train and bus pass, originally from private rail companies
pointo cādo, points card
Poppoya, immensely popular railway story-cycle and film originally written by Asada Jirō

rāmen, Chinese style noodles
Ran, Kurosawa film based on *King Lear*
Rashōmon, classic Akira Kurosawa film
romaji, roman or western alphabetization (as here)
romance car, Odakyū special express train
rōnin, samurai without master or lord. Also used to identify high-school graduates who have taken a year off before entering university in order to study for university entrance examinations.
Ryōgoku kokugikan, Tokyo sumo headquarters and arena
ryokan, traditional Japanese inn

sake, brewed rice 'wine'

sakura, cherry blossom

san bon jime, three-times over ritual handclap. Always used at the
  end of a meeting or party. Jime is a form of shime which is from
  shimeru – to close.

Sanrio Purolan, Tama-town games and show-time centre for children

sashimi, meticulously sliced raw fish usually eaten with dipping
  sauce.

seijin no hi, coming of age day

seisan ki, fare adjustment machine

sembei, rice cracker

Setagaya Boroichi, twice a year Setagaya flee market

Setagaya Line, branch line connecting to the Odakyū Line

shaden, shrine complex

shamisen, three-stringed banjo-like instrument

shika, deer

Shinjuku-eki, central Tokyo station

shinkansen, bullet train

shinto, traditional Nature-centred Japanese belief system

Shiraishi, Kazuko, well-known and controversial performance poet

shisa kanko, system of gestures and calls intended to keep station personnel alert

shōgun, military commander or general

shokutaku, work taken on by retirees who are being re-hired on a
  full-time or part-time basis.

SMAP, well-known all-male Japanese pop group

soba, buckwheat noodle

sugoi, great, excellent

suica, all-purpose rail and bus passes, originally from JR, and used in
  the greater Kanto region

sumimasen, excuse me

sumire, violet (flower)

sumo, Japan's signature sport, traditional wrestling

sumo terminology:

  banzuke, sumo ranking list

  basho, tournament, six principal per year

  chonmage, top-knot

  dohyō, circular fight-ring on clay circumscribed by rope

  gunbai, originally a war fan, used to indicate time to wrestle

  gyoji, umpire (in the dohyō)

  hyogōshi, clappers

makunouchi dohyō-iri, ring-entering ceremony conducted by upper-division wrestlers

mawashi, belt

mono ii, judges' consultation in case of disputed result

okuri-taoshi, rear push-out

oshidashi, ring push out

ōzeki, rank next to the top Grand Champion

rikishi, wrestler (s)

sanyaku, jūryo, makushita, sumo ranks or divisions

shiko, foot stamping ritual to help limber up the wrestler

shinpan, judge (seated round the dohyō). Composed mainly of stable-masters who themselves are former wrestlers.

shitenage, under arm throw-down, as against ūwatenage, over-arm thrown down

tachiai, opening charge

unryū-gata dohyō, opening ceremony performed by the yokozuna

yobidashi, sumo official who calls out wrestlers' names

yokozuna, top-of-the-ladder Grand Champion

yorikiri, ring push out

yotsu, mutual grip or clasp

sushi, vinegared rice with sliced raw fish or other accompaniments

sutorappu, literally straps. Medallions and like usually hung from phones or bags

tai, white fish. Sea bream or red snapper

Takashimaya, Japanese department chain-store

Tama Nyūtaun, Tama New Town

Tama Sentah Parutenon, Tama Centre Parthenon

Tamagawa, Tama River

tarento, from talent. TV or other entertainment personality

tatami, mat, straw carpet

tayū, bunraku narrator

tempura, seafood or vegetable dipped in light batter and fried

tetchan, boy train enthusiast

Tetsudō Hakubutsukan, railway museum in Saitama opened in 2007. Also railway station.

Tezuka, Osamu (1928-89), leading manga artist

Thirty-Six Views of Mount Fuji (1831-). Key sequence of ukiyo-e prints by Hiroshige

Todai, Tokyo University

tofu, bean curd made of coagulated soy milk

toire, toilet

Tokai Genshiryoku Hatsudensho, Tokai Nuclear Power Plant

Tokyo Joshi Daigaku, abbreviated to Tonjo, Tokyo Woman's
  Christian University

Tokyo Shimbun, Tokyo-centred daily newspaper

torii, shrine-gate, T-shaped, marking the sacred from the secular or
  profane

tsuyu, dipping soy-based sauce

ukiyo-e, literally pictures of the floating world. Vintage Japanese
  woodblock print art-form.

unagi, eel

wa, peace, harmony, balance

wainrisuto, wine list

washiki, Japanese style toilet

Wel Park, sign for the Welcia Kanto Company, a drugstore
  chain

yakitori, grilled and skewered chicken

yaki-zakana, grilled fish

yakuza, organized crime gangster

Yakusho, Koji, well known Japanese screen actor

Yamada, Masahiro, contemporary life-form artist

Yamashita koen, Yamashita park at the Yokohama city waterfront

Yodobashi Camera, Japanese electronics chain

Yokohama Chūkagai, Yokohama Chinatown

Yokohama gaikokujin bochi, Yokohama Foreign Cemetery

yōkoso, welcome

yokozuna, grand champion sumo wrestler

Yomiuri Shimbun, Japanese daily newspaper

yoshi, pronounced 'yosh', OK (said by train drivers and
  personnel)

Yoyogi-Uehara, Odakyū Line station connecting to the Chiyoda
  Line

yūchi ginkō, Post Office bank

yūsenseki, priority seating on trains and buses

zenrin-mon, Friendship Gate (to Yokohama Chinatown)

zōri, slippers